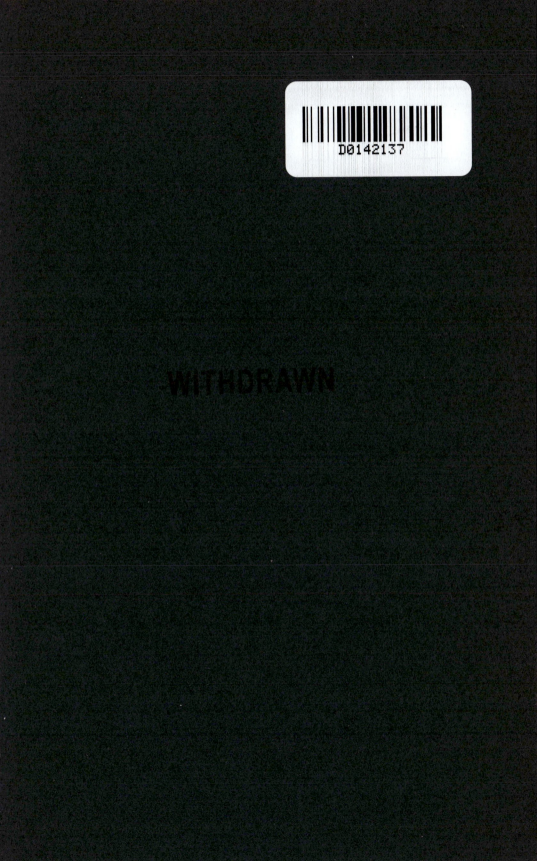

D0142137

Economics,
Politics,
and
The Age
of Inflation

Paul Mattick

Economics, Politics, and The Age of Inflation

M.E.Sharpe INC.

WHITE PLAINS, N.Y.

The first five essays were originally published in German and were translated by Michel Vale.

Published simultaneously as Vol. VII, no. 3 of
International Journal of Politics.

Library of Congress Catalog Card Number: 78-68044
International Standard Book Number: 0-87332-123-5

Printed in the United States of America

Contents

Preface

Commenting on the proceedings of the 1977 convention of the American Economic Association, an editorial in *The New York Times* lamented the fact that "today's economists seem mere dabblers in the sweep of intellectual history. They may be richly rewarded by business for their stabs at forecasting and their analyses of government regulation or floating exchange rates. But where are the attacks on the biggest problem of our time: achieving growth without spiraling inflation? . . . Most economists were dismal scientists when they arrived. Despite the drinks and the chats, they were unchanged when they left three days later."

The economists are in a dismal state precisely because they look upon their discipline as a science whereas it is actually no more than a sophisticated apology for the social and economic *status quo*. They evidently do not perceive the real nature of their profession and thus are deeply disturbed by the growing discrepancy between their theories and reality. Because the "economic weather" had favored them for such a long time, they may have really imagined that the mathematization of economics had turned their preoccupations with price and market relations into a positive science. As Thomas Balogh remarked in a paper delivered in 1975 at University College, London, "there were as many equations as there were unknowns, and these it was claimed could capture reality and enable objective and positive advice to be given to political leaders. Inequality would be diminished and individuals protected against exceptional hardship. Economics would, moreover, produce testable theses, and enable the production of 'policy menus,' which would provide us with a solid basis for scientific decision-making and quantified 'trade-offs,' i.e., in plain English, 'choices.' The consumption function, the accelerator, Okun's 'law' of the relation of income to employment, the Phillips curve link-ing wages to unemployment, linear programming, etc. — now all shown up for the nonsense that they were — would at last have raised the economist to the level of physicist. How long ago this all seems now."

Economics is no longer seen as an exact science. As an "inexact" one its predictive powers are highly questionable, thus disqualifying the "stabs at forecasting" that were to justify its existence. Predictions are "probability statements" that commit the forecaster to nothing at all. His guess is as good as any other, for no one knows how the dice will fall. Economics is back at its starting point — submission to Adam Smith's "invisible hand" —without the consoling illusion of its beneficiary results. However, the dilemma of economics is still not traced to the economic system itself but to the incompleteness of the science of economics, which has not as yet found ways and means to make the demonstrably unworkable economy workable.

The current, more direct concern of economics is the combination of economic stagnation with inflation, which destroyed both Keynesian theory and the neo-Keynesian synthesis that had passed as the standard theory of economics. It is to this aspect of the matter that the following collection of articles devotes itself, taking the point of view of critical political economy.

Although these articles must speak for themselves, it should be pointed out that they were written for different occasions and that they address different audiences. It was thus inevitable that they repeat some basic statements without which each item would in itself be less comprehensible. But this necessity may prove an asset rather than an annoyance, since it shows up the interconnections between the phenomenal world of capitalism and its underlying social production relations.

With the exception of one, all the articles relate to the main issues of today, namely, the role of government, or the state, in economic affairs with reference to both the so-called mixed economies and the state-capitalist systems. The exception deals with the Great Depression of 1929 and the New Deal, which initiated the era of large-scale governmental intervention in the economy of the United States.

P. M.

Economics,
Politics,
and
The Age
of Inflation

1

The Crisis of the Mixed Economy

To understand the present economic situation and where it is going, one must take a look into the events of the recent past. Developments since the end of World War II have taken place entirely within a new kind of capitalism calling itself a "mixed economy." This implies state economic interventions that differ from the interventionist policies of the past century in extent but not so much in the means applied.

State interventions under a mixed economy find their reasons as well as their limits in the conditions of existence and accumulation of private capital. Quite apart from the instruments of power that the state uses to secure social stability on the domestic front and to support national interests in international competition, it has always exercised economic functions as well, e.g., as a means of obtaining revenue (customs policies and state monopolies over certain branches of industry, etc.) or of creating the general conditions of production the burden for which private capital either did not or could not assume itself (e.g., construction of roads, harbors, railroads, posts, and so on, i..e., what in the economic jargon is called infrastructure).

Thus in limited measure the state is also a producer of surplus value and is therefore able to pay for a portion of its expenditures with its own profits. To the extent that the production of state enterprises enters into general competition, it differs in no way from private production; and the state share in total surplus value depends on the mass of capital it invests and on the average rate of profit. State monopoly over certain products and services may lead to monopolistic profits, but this is only another form of consumer taxation.

For historical and other reasons the relationship between state and private production is changeable and, moreover, varies from country to country. State enterprises may be turned over to private concerns, and private enterprises may be nationalized; the state may be a shareholder in private concerns or keep them alive through subsidies. The interpenetration of private and state production occurs in a variety of combinations, and the state share need not be restricted to the infrastructure. In the industrially developing countries state participation in production is often relatively extensive, as for example, in Italy, an archetypal country in this respect, where state-owned production[1] competing with private capital represents 15 percent of total production. Yet no matter how much state production may expand, it can never be more than a minor fraction of total production if it is not to call into question the very existence of a market economy. In all countries, therefore, a "mixed economy," to the extent that it is a mixture, leaves the private enterprise nature of the economy intact.

Even an increase in state production through expansion of the infrastructure can change nothing, since this expansion takes place within the framework of capitalist accumulation, which reproduces the relationship between state and private production in consonance with accumulation needs. Expanding automobile production entails the construction of new highways, and growing air traffice requires more airports, etc., if expansion of the economy as a whole is not to lag behind the infrastructure. Though it is correct to say that state-organized creation of the general conditions of production benefits private capital, albeit quite unevenly, this does not mean that it improves the profitability of capital beyond the costs of the infrastructure. Since the costs of the infrastructure are borne by private capital, the infrastructure depends on the profitability of capital, not vice versa.

The general conditions of production demonstrate the unsocial nature of capitalist production, namely, that it is impossible for the general needs of society to be taken care of by private production. The capitalist ideal would be for every form of production, even production for the infrastructure, to be run privately. As, however, this is in practical terms impossible, capital leaves it to the state to balance private production with social production. Capital must still, however, bear the costs of this production, and it is therefore little interested in expanding the infrastructure beyond the narrow scope it finds useful. The result is that, in general, infrastructural production lags behind production for the market — a state often lamented in the economic literature as an irremediable contradiction between private wealth and public poverty.

In a crisis situation state-induced production is not primarily production for further expansion of the infrastructure in anticipation of and preparation for expected future capitalist accumulation. Its purpose is to create jobs immediately, with a view toward increasing general demand. In order not to compound further the existing problems of private production, state-induced production must concentrate on things outside of the market and on public spending, which may partly go toward expanding the general conditions of production and partly be used up in "public consumption." This type of state-induced production must be distinguished from the state production that already exists, whether it is geared to the creation of the general conditions of production or to the general market.

Private production is not on that account driven out of business by state production; the latter is merely a policy undertaken to combat crisis. It is financed by a state budget deficit, even if in the end this only means an added tax burden apportioned to the private sector over the long term. The state must strive to expand total production beyond its own production capacities, which is why when we investigate the effect of state-induced production, normal state production may be disregarded.

The state does not have any means of production of its own to cover the additional state-induced production. Even for production of the general conditions of production, the state must for the most part rely on the services of private enterprise, which are then paid for from taxes and state loans. To the extent that the general conditions of production are a prerequisite for capitalist production for profit, their cost is objectively a part of the costs of capitalist production. Where this is not the case, the costs of state-induced production must be subtracted from total surplus value and cannot be included in either capitalist consumption or capitalist accumulation.

Crisis brings capitalist accumulation to a halt, and at the level of the market this shows up as overproduction and unemployment. Crisis occurs because profits are not sufficient to meet the expansion needs of the existing capital structure. In this situation any further deductions from the mass of surplus value, which is already inadequate, can only worsen the predicament of capital. Any increase in demand through public works projects must therefore be financed by state loans, and the additional state-induced production shows up as a mounting public debt.

That government spending is for the most part covered by deductions from the mass of surplus value is brought to light by taxation. Capital is always demanding a reduction in its tax burden. However, it is not necessary to balance the state budget every year; debts incurred during a depression may be paid off during times of prosperity. If they are not, the interest on state loans constitutes an additional tax burden which, however, may be stabilized at a low level by expanding production. As long as social production expands faster than the state debt, the latter poses no serious problem for the economy. If the opposite is the case, the state debt becomes a burden on the economy and another obstacle to the resumption of accumulation.

State-induced production to make up for deficient demand was initially conceived as a temporary relief measure for waiting out the depression on a safer note until the next business upswing, and it was therefore used only in limited measure. If capital could not create the conditions for a new economic upswing from its own resources, expansion of the infrastructure through public works would be of little use to it. Two empty harbors are no better than one, and two highways without traffic no better than one without traffic. During the Great Depression public works reduced unemployment but did not eliminate it, and the long depression ended with World War II, not with a new economic upswing. It took the war to bring about full employment without capitalist accumulation. Capital was not only destroyed in terms of values, it was also destroyed physically. In the United States as well accumulation came to a halt when about half of production went into "public consumption," that is, wartime production. Nonetheless this arrest of accumulation and the enormous destruction of capital created the conditions for the economic boom of the postwar period.

Periodic crises have been a part of capitalism as long as it has existed, but because capital does develop, the periods of crisis differ, if not in essence, at least in outward form. The postwar boom was such a surprise because it came right on the heels of the long years of depression, which had deeply shaken confidence in the ability of capital to survive and grow. How was this boom to be explained? The Marxist theory of crisis explains it by the fact that capital was once more able to restore the vital link between profit and accumulation which had been lost. The worldwide destruction of capital values and the changes it wrought in the structure of capital, together with the expansion of surplus value made possible by technical improvements in the means of production, permitted the capital that had survived and the capital that had been newly created to achieve a rate of profit sufficient for capital to expand. Thus the new boom, like all those in the past, was seen as the outcome of the crisis situation preceding it, which in turn was seen as a disproportionality between the creation of profit and the accumulation requirements of capital.

At issue here was the contradiction, inherent in the production of surplus value, that the amount of capital invested in wages decreases relative to the amount of capital invested in means of production, so that total surplus value accordingly diminishes relative to total capital. Capital accumulation is not only a necessity born of competition, it also derives from the never ending struggle against the tendential decline in the rate of profit inherent in the capitalist mode of production, and this struggle grows more difficult as accumulation proceeds. While surplus value is, on the one hand, increased by accumulation, and on the other hand, accumulation causes the rate of profit to decline, at any particular time actual profits may fail to reach the level required for further accumulation. Since Marx describes this process in *Capital*, we need not repeat the description here. It will suffice to point out that prosperity and depression constitute the contradictory outward garb of the development of the social forces of production under conditions of capital production.

Bourgeois economic theory sees these events in a different light. For it price relations on the market, not production and production relations, are the essential factors to be considered.

7

The great crisis of 1929 forced the abandonment of the equilibrium theory of a self-regulating economy. The crisis was in-
terpreted as based on a lack of effective demand due to a decline
in consumer needs, showing up as a lack of new investments and
hence unemployment. But this peculiar explanation aside, bourgeois theory also agreed that production had to be stimulated if
the crisis, which seemed to have set in permanently, was to be
overcome. If this was not achieved of itself from profit-deter-
mined market relations, state interventions could be used to stimulate production — the full employment of the war years was a
persuasive example of this. Since it seemed that capital was no
longer capable of extracting itself from the crisis by means of its
own resources, and since the continuation and deepening of the
crisis began to undermine social stability, both bourgeois prac-
titioners and theoreticians opted for an interventionist policy to
prime the pump, as it were, and eliminate unemployment.

If profitable expansion of production was not possible, expansion independent of profit was; and although this could not
promote capital accumulation directly, it could perhaps get production going again. Production even without profit seemed better
than standing still, especially when it was tied to the expectation
that it would provide the impetus for the resumption of the accumulation process.

The multiplier effect theory was invented to substantiate this
reasoning. The notion of a multiplier had appeared before,[2] although it had not been taken as seriously or formulated as precisely as by R. F. Kahn and J. M. Keynes. Their particular formulation aside, it is obvious that any significant new investment, no
matter of what kind, must increase production if it is not immediately offset by the withdrawal of other investments, and that,
moreover, this added production will also generate some surplus
value. If the additional surplus value is reinvested in means of production and labor power, capital accumulation also increases.

But surplus value is transformed into additional capital only
when existing capital is profitable enough to justify further capitalist expansion. The crisis was a sign that capital was not profitable
enough to allow for more accumulation. And since state production yields no profit, its effect on profitable production in the pri-

vate sector can only very marginally increase total surplus value. Although surplus value expands in the private sector as a result of state-induced production, this growth itself must be measured against the production costs of the latter to determine if it can actually influence the social surplus value positively.

To avoid misunderstandings we should point out that just as creditors of the state debt obtain their interest, so do the private enterprises engaged in state-induced production receive an average, and often an above-average, profit. These interests and profits, however, are not generated via the market but through state purchases of the output the state itself set into motion, i.e., the added output, which includes surplus value, is "exchanged" for a capitalist surplus value in money form that had been created at an earlier period. The money which flows from the hands of capital to the state returns from whence it came in an amount commensurate with the volume of state-induced production. In other words, surplus value that was already part of capital is "exchanged" for state-induced output.

Money becomes capital by being transformed into means of production and labor power used for the production of surplus value; this process, which constitutes capital accumulation, is reproduced continuously. In themselves money and means of production have none of the properties of capital; they first acquire such properties through the production of surplus value. Money and means of production lie idle during times of crisis because nowhere would their employment yield sufficient surplus value. But though they are not utilized, they still remain private property that the state must appropriate to begin state-induced production.

The latter comes under the heading of neither private consumption nor capitalist accumulation. However, consumption also expands with production via the surplus value "realized" through state-induced production and through the wages of the workers employed in producing the increased output, as well as through the effects of state-induced production on production in general. The final product, however, which ends up in public consumption, still embodies the totality of its production costs. If, for example, the American space research program costs $20 billion, this sum represents a portion of the state budget that must be raised by society as a whole. It cannot be capitalized, whatever ultimate technical benefit may accrue to commodity-producing capital from the achievements of space research. It must also be taken into account that while in capitalist production existing capital is amortized within a certain period by the commodities it produces, and in this way survives to expand by way of the surplus value, under state-induced production, production of surplus value and amortization of capital can take place only through the state budget, i.e., via the surplus value extracted from the private sector.

However, state-induced production and private production are so complexly interwoven that no clear-cut line can be drawn between them. Enterprises operate in both sectors at the same time and make as little distinction as does economic theory between income coming from state-induced production and that accruing from production for the private sector. National income is calculated on the basis of total production, without regard for the origin or the destination of its individual components. But if the state budget grows more rapidly than total income, the gap between profitless and profitable production widens. The fact that in the capitalist countries about one third of the national income goes into the state budget and is supplemented by deficit financing shows that more and more of the total surplus value is being kept out of private capital formation.

Conversely, if national income grows more rapidly than the state budget and the state debt, it means that the proportion of state-induced production within total production is on the decrease, and that capitalist accumulation may be correspondingly enlarged. It must, however, be remembered that at issue here is a state-induced production undertaken to compensate for sagging private production, and not just the expansion of state spending in itself, which may also have other reasons, e.g., the exigencies of war or imperialist policies.

The imperialist rivalries of nationally organized capital have also given birth to a state apparatus which, in close collaboration with the capital entities benefiting from state-induced production, has established itself in a relatively independent position of power it secures by maintaining and expanding its control over the economy. Thus it is not always clear to what extent continuing expansion of the state budget derives from the objective need for state-induced production and to what extent it is forced on society by special interests allied to the state.

By far the greater part of state-induced production is in the war and armaments industry, i.e., production for public consumption. This production is at once a cause and the expression of the low rate of capital expansion. Specifically, on the one hand it can be claimed that public consumption detracts from accumulation, yet it is also arguable that without it economic activity would be even more depressed than it actually is. Since war and armaments have so far in fact been inseparable from capital, it is impossible to ascertain to what extent curbs on state-induced production would further capital accumulation or diminish productive activity.

Though this question may resist an empirical answer, we can nonetheless explore it theoretically. Assuming that there are no objective obstacles in the way of capitalist accumulation, which could grow by the available mass of surplus value, any loss of surplus value through public consumption would mean less accumulation. In principle the less consumption there is of any kind, the more can be accumulated. This may be the case, but not necessarily so. The profit requirements of further accumulation may surpass the actual surplus value obtained at the expense of consumption because of an existing discrepancy between the existing capital structure and the given rate of exploitation, so that only a change in the structure of capital and an increase in labor productivity can expand the value of capital. Under such conditions curbs on public consumption would have no effect on accumulation. A capitalist crisis would then be needed to effect the social changes under which capital could continue the accumulation process.

The resurgence of economic activity following World War II was not due to state-induced production alone; a far weightier factor was the fact that despite increased public consumption, capital was once again able to emerge from the depression to begin a new era of prosperity. As already stated, the changes wrought in the international structure of capital by war and depression, rapid technological advances, and a cutback in consumption on a world scale led to a high rate of accumulation in several countries at once. The restoration of the war-devastated infrastructure and the resumption of capital reproduction, neglected during the war, together with a steady, relatively high level of public consumption necessitated by continuing imperialist power politics, produced the "economic miracles" in the reconstruction countries and saw American capital expand across the globe. But all this says no more than that the surplus value generated in production was sufficient to meet the needs of both capitalist accumulation and public spending.

But capitalism's regaining of its own internal dynamic had to contend with the theory of a generally static capitalism, developed during the depression, according to which full employment could only be achieved through state intervention. The fact that some countries were approaching while others, for the time at least, were enjoying full employment was proof enough for the "new economics" that the state does in fact possess the power to eliminate the capitalist business cycle. By means of monetary and fiscal policies it was possible at any time, it was asserted, for the state to transform a flagging economy into its opposite and to maintain employment at any desired level. Two ways were presumably available to do this: indirect, through easing credit terms to the private sector, and direct, through public spending made possible by deficit financing. And since the new upswing had been marred by periods of recession that were overcome by stepping up state spending, the view that a market economy could be steered by the state and that capitalist crises were things of the past set in more firmly.

If the cause of crises lies in an arrest of the accumulation process, which occurs when the portion of surplus value not earmarked for consumption is not invested in more means of production and labor power, production and employment must necessarily decrease. The repercussions on the overall workings of capital, however, go far beyond the actual cutback effected in production. The extremely intricate market relations cause the cutbacks in production to widen into a general crisis. State-induced augmentation of production and its effect on market relations can doubtless check an ensuing economic recession, provided it is a limited one easily dealt with by limited means. And indeed, the snags that have arisen periodically in the economy during the postwar period have been overcome by countervailing measures from the state. It does not follow, however, that this will continue to be the case for all time to come. It tells us only that the beginning signs of crisis have appeared in a situation in which a fall-off in private production could still be offset by compensatory expansion of public expenditures. Actually, the extremely long period of depression before World War II was followed by an extremely long period of boom whose internal fluctuations the state had been able to control in a positive fashion. These were fluctuations occurring in a general upswing and not in a general crisis resulting from overaccumulation. We have not yet had enough experience to enable us to determine whether it is within the means of the state under capitalism to cope with such a crisis, although the limits to state intervention are clearly discernible.

The surplus value from past production periods, which either remains in money form or is embodied in idle means of production because of the crisis, has lost its capital function. It can regain this function only via the production of profit. When this possibility is closed, the state is able to appropriate uninvested money and thus employ unused means of production. But this does not restore their capital function. The money and means of production thereby mobilized are transformed into products that are used up in public consumption and hence drop out of the reproduction process of total capital.

Whatever else may arise from this process, production geared to public consumption ceases being surplus-value production in the form of additional money and means of production. The surplus value of the larger capital employed is now smaller relative to the total capital. A portion of the already accumulated capital has thereby not only lost its capital function, it also ceases being unused capital. Whereas, however, the destruction of capital during a crisis alters the relationship between total profits and total capital in such a way that the reduced value of capital raises the rate of profit at the expense of the destroyed capital, in the case of state-induced production for public consumption, the profit and interest claims of the money and means of production therein employed remain unchanged — as if this kind of production was actually production for profit and as if the destruction of capital in public consumption had not occurred. Thus in the end this kind of production does not result in the improvement in the rate of profit that ensues during a crisis as a result of the destruction of capital values and the claims on the social profit attached to them; rather capital is destroyed while its profit claims, which can only be met out of the total social surplus value, are maintained.

That portion of the total profits of the private sector which accrues to capital entities participating in state-induced production must be subtracted from total profits as it derives from tax revenues; this entails a decrease in the profit rate of productive, i.e., profitable, capital and hence a setback for accumulation. However, these capital entities can compensate for their diminished profits by raising prices, thereby shifting the burden of the costs of state-induced production to society.

Thus this stepped-up public spending takes on the form of price inflation resulting from the attempt to dump the costs of combating the crisis on the population at large, i.e., the working population.

The profitability of private capital is thereby maintained without assuming a further accumulation of capital. All that is accomplished by this route is that more workers are put to work at the expense of the total income of the working population. This is achieved by inflationary means rather than by the deflationary path chosen in the past, which progressively increased unemployment. But since there are definite limits to the burdens the workers can bear, and the drop in real wages due to price inflation meets with their resistance, the financing of public spending at the expense of the working class sooner or later reaches a limit it cannot exceed. From this point onward public consumption can only continue to grow at the expense of capital.

If capital accumulation is not resumed, the crisis deepens and unemployment grows. State-induced production must then expand if it is to continue in its compensatory role. The effect is growing pressure on the profit rate of productive capital, which makes the resumption of accumulation ever more difficult, thereby prolonging the depression. If the expansion of state-induced production does not stop, it too becomes a factor aggravating the crisis, although it had originally been intended as a means to beat it, and indeed for a time actually did function as such. But it had this effect only with regard to total material production, without enhancing capital accumulation. It did not yield enough profits to accomplish more than an increase of production through decreasing profitability of capital. As depression continues, even this ability will be lost; as state-induced production expands, private production must decrease and, as a consequence, will lose the ability to cover increased public spending.

The cyclical movement of capital has so far prevented a crisis from setting in permanently, and there is no empirical evidence that profitless production is possible only at the expense of profitable production and is therefore limited by the latter. The point to be gained here, however, is the insight that capital cannot accumulate without sufficient profit. An increase in production without a corresponding increase in profit is of no use to capital as capital, even though for political reasons it may be of use to capitalist society. Even the immediate positive effect state-induced production has on the private sector may be canceled by the enlarged continuation of compensatory state production. If capital does not autonomously move on to resume accumulation on its own terms, the impetus given to it by state-induced production will gradually lose its driving force, until it finally becomes an obstacle to accumulation.

Production in the state sector is tied to the profits of the private sector, and its expansion is contingent on the latter's increase. If this does not occur, the situation of the private sector can only continue to grow worse, until it makes further expansion of the state sector objectively impossible. But private capital, which still controls society even in a "mixed economy," would stop expansion in the public sector long before it reached its objective limits. State-induced production is allowed to expand only to the extent this can be borne by capital, i.e., so long as it does not call into question the continued existence and growth of capital. It may therefore only be regarded as a temporary measure that at a specific point in capitalist decline must be stopped, thereby ceasing to be a factor working against this decline.

Actually, and apart from war production, the expansion of state-induced production has taken place not while capitalism was standing relatively still but during an upswing, which was viewed as the fruit of a mixed economy. But the reality of the situation was just the opposite. The upswing resulting from the restoration of profitability was large enough so that even though public consumption continued to grow steadily, a state of relative prosperity, seen in capitalist terms, was achieved. Since the task of state economic policy was to expand lagging production, the economic upswing should have resulted in a contraction of state-induced production; this, however, was not the case. To be sure, relative to the overall growth in production, the expansion of the state sector proceeded at a slower pace, the practice of budgetary deficits was curtailed, and the size of these deficits was reduced; the state deficit, however, continued to rise, although more slowly than before. As far as expansion of the private sector was concerned, this situation seemed to be ideal not only from the standpoint of current economic theory but also for capital itself, as well as for those with vested interests in public spending.

But the capital growth that went on independently despite relatively high public consumption remained in large measure under the influence of state economic policy, i.e., its monetary and credit, if not so much its fiscal, aspects. The whole of capitalist production had long been based on the credit mechanism. But credit not only remained dependent on the maintenance of a given level of profitability, it was also limited in its expansion by state controls over money and credit, although these limits were flexible. Through credit production can be expanded beyond the limits to which it is subject if there is no credit. Thus additional state-induced production is made possible by credit, i.e., by state debt, and similarly production in the private sector can be expanded by widening the credit mechanism. Through its power to create money and extend credit, the state is able to expand or contract the basis of credit in various ways. The credit volume and interest rates can in large measure be controlled, bank lending stimulated, and production accordingly expanded by a cheap money policy, by increasing the money supply, by the discount policy of the central bank, and by the "open market policy," as it is called.

The boom was accompanied by rapid growth in the money supply and in credit, which served in two respects. First, it helped to expand production, and second, it effected a reapportionment of social income in favor of capital. Every expansion of credit tends toward inflation, and a systematic, state-encouraged money and credit expansion is particularly inflationary. To top all this off there is also the inflationary influence of profitless state-induced production. But inflation, which at first only crept along as the boom proceeded apace, was accepted as the price that had to be paid for economic growth and was thought to be manageable. In any case growth with inflation was to be preferred to a stagnant, deflationary economy; indeed, it was argued, the inflation that went along with growth was only the expression of the secret, discovered by the "new economics," of permanent full employment and economic stability.

Actually, the increasing rate of inflation pointed to an internal weakness of the boom; namely, it allowed the state neither to cut off its expansive money and credit policy nor to cut back on public spending to any significant extent. Every contraction of credit and every reduction in the money supply, and indeed every decrease in public consumption, had an immediate negative effect on the course of the economy and were discarded in favor of a resumption of an inflationary policy. Thus the waves of prosperity that followed World War II turned out to be movements that depended to some extent on state monetary and fiscal policies, although in a few countries they had been able to raise general demand to the level of full employment.

Obviously money and credit policies can themselves change nothing with regard to profitability or insufficient profits. Profits come only from production, from the surplus value produced by workers. If the surplus value is sufficient for expanded reproduction of capital, a period of capitalist prosperity sets in. But if capitalist expansion must be primed by money and credit policies to stimulate demand, it is not long before it becomes clear that something is wrong with production for profit. The expansion of credit has always been taken as a sign of a coming crisis, in the sense that it reflected the attempt of individual capital entities to expand despite sharpening competition, and hence to survive the crisis. Credit has always been a means of capital concentration whenever profitability falls. Although the expansion of credit has staved off crisis for a short time, it has never prevented it, since ultimately it is the real relationship between total profits and the needs of social capital to expand in value which is the decisive factor, and that cannot be altered by credit.

It is not credit but only the increase in production made possible by it that increases surplus value. It is then the rate of exploitation which determines credit expansion. To stimulate the general demand, the expansive state-imposed money and credit policies must increase profit. If profit does not increase relative to the invested capital and increased production, yet the level of production made possible by credit is to be sustained, the distribution of the social product between capital and labor must be altered to ensure the profitability of capital. If prices rise faster than wages, then what could not be extracted from the workers in production is taken from them in the circulation process. This is at once the cause and the consequence of the expansion of money and credit, so that an inflationary growth in profits appears as accelerating inflation.

To the extent that an expansive monetary and credit policy served to increase profits, it furthered capital production, although it was at the same time a sign of inadequate profitability, albeit concealed, and added to the state debt a private debt that was many times greater. The steady growth of debt could be sustained only if capital accumulation could progress uninterrupted by way of credit expansion. Once accumulation stops, the expansion of production through monetary and credit policies stops as well, and their progressive effect is transformed into its opposite. But since accumulation entails a falling rate of profit, management of the economy by way of monetary and credit policies and by means of state-induced production must eventually find its end in the contradictions of the accumulation process.

Another weakness inherent in the postwar boom was the fact that it was unevenly distributed among the various capitalist countries, to say nothing of the negative effects it had on the underdeveloped nations. Although the latter consequence was favorable to growth in the capitalist countries, in that it guaranteed a cheap source of raw materials to the developed countries, it was also a sign that the boom was not strong enough to envelop the entire world economy and thereby become general. The accumulation rate was high only in the Western European countries and Japan; in the United States it remained below its historical average, while the rest of the world for the most part stagnated. But the pace of investments promoted by government policies in Western Europe and Japan did bring about an exceptional and long-lasting prosperity. The overall standard of living rose as a consequence of a rapid increase in labor productivity and the particular structure of European and Japanese capital. Although the high growth rates hit snags from time to time, setbacks were quickly overcome. In the United States, however, full employment and full utilization of production capacity were not achieved.

The creeping inflation that accompanied the economic boom also was the vehicle that carried it along; but it was also a sign of an immanent contradiction insofar as continuance of the boom was contingent on an accelerating inflation rate. Inflation is an expression of inadequate profits that must be offset by price and money policies. Therefore in the developing capitalist countries, Brazil, for example, inflation is the measure chosen to bring profits into line with the pace of accumulation, i.e., to accelerate expansion at the expense of working-class consumption, to promote exports, or to do both at once. Thus under any circumstances inflation spells the need for higher profits, whether this be the need of a particular capital entity to obtain profits or a general effort to add steam to accumulation.

Capitalist accumulation is a struggle between labor and capital, and within certain definite limits this struggle determines how much surplus value is produced. At the same time however, accumulation is capital's competitive struggle at the national and international levels to determine how surplus value is to be apportioned. Monetary policy affects both these contests. Inflation makes labor cheaper, which improves the ability of national capital to compete, although only when the inflation rates vary from country to country, which in turn is dependent on the class struggle in the different countries and on the particular economic posisition of each nation within the world economy as a whole. The international struggle of competition is also waged over monetary policy. At the same time, however, the bourgeoisie is interested in easing competition, so that attempts are made continually to bring some order into monetary and credit relations through international agreements.

The capitalist economy is a world economy whose existence assumes competition. Competition drives capital concentration forward both nationally and internationally. But the progressive elimination of competition at the national level only makes all the contradictions inherent in the system more acute, since accumulation, expressed in concentration, intensifies the pressure on the profit rate and hence harshens all social conflicts; in like manner, rather than being a sign of diminishing capitalist antagonisms, the international concentration of capital merely gives these antagonisms a more overtly imperialist character, as evidenced so far by two world wars and a number of localized wars.

Like the capitalist crisis imperialist rivalry is both the cause and effect of the capitalist economy and cannot be separated from capital's need to accumulate. Thus the postwar boom must not be seen just abstractly, as a consequence of capital's cyclic movement, but as the result as well of changes wrought in the political forces by World War II and the effects these changes had on international competition. The boom was also in large measure determined by the rivalries emerging among the victorious powers, who were faced with the task of consolidating their conquests and further extending their positions of power.

There can be no question that the relatively rapid reconstruction of the capitalist economies of Western Europe and Japan was primed initially by American aid, offered out of imperialistic considerations; not only were credits granted, but the export potential of these countries received a powerful shot in the arm from the far-ranging imperialist ambitions of the United States. The relatively low rate of accumulation in the United States and the reduced profit rate occasioned by war and armaments production forced American capital to export capital to countries where more abundant profits awaited them, which further augmented their already inflated rates of investment. But this feverish activity, together with the unabating expansion of credit in the United States, caused inflation to spread to one country after another, until it finally became a world phenomenon.

As economic growth in Japan and Western Europe proceeded, the relations of these countries with the world market, and with the United States in particular, changed. The labor productivity gap between the United States and the other capitalist countries, which depended on the volume of capital invested and on the ends to which it was put, grew narrower, and America's dominant share in world trade shrunk correspondingly, until the United States found itself with a negative balance of trade on its hands. The balance of payments had already been negative for quite some time because of the cost of imperialist politics and the initial one-way flow of capital exports. Thus European expansion was partly made possible by America's negative balance of payments and attendant inflationary monetary and credit policies. American monetary policy became an instrument of imperialist expansion not only to secure U.S. spheres of influence in world power politics but also to enlarge direct investments in other countries, especially in growing Western Europe.

From the standpoint of the world economy as a whole, it makes no difference in what nation capital is accumulated, even though from a national perspective this same process will look different. As long as capital can move freely, it invests where it expects the highest profits are to be had and accordingly stimulates general economic activity in favor of the invested capital. Since all capitalist countries export and import capital, one can only say apropos of the extraordinarily large volume of American capital export that the United States merely took advantage of the existing opportunity to gain a foothold in other countries, and that this opportunity emerged from the peculiarities of the postwar situation and from state monetary and credit policies. The direct foreign investments and the volume in which they occurred only accelerated the general inflation that was already under way in the United States. Nonetheless these processes, if they did not contain the secret to the boom itself, in any event were the expression of its pronounced inflationary character.

All the ups and downs of the most recent past and present on the market throughout the world economy are traceable to these processes. It is only the market, of course, to which capital can relate and to which it must react in one way or another. It is also only market processes which the state seeks to influence in whatever ways it deems beneficial or necessary.

Yet the underlying state of things in the sphere of profitable production remains closed to scrutiny and practical action, although it is the factor that determines the course of accumulation. By its nature the capitalist mode of production precludes empirical insight into the production relations of the society as a whole, and the market becomes the point of reference for all capitalist decisions, although these decisions are still subject to the influence of processes taking place in the production sphere. They still must be implemented at the level of the market, however, on the terms set by competition, so that one is left with no way of knowing whether such decisions correspond to realities in the production sphere. Whatever the circumstances, all movements of individual capital, and hence of capital as a totality, are aimed at maintaining a state of expanding profits and hence correspond to processes in the production sphere, without this guaranteeing that they will be successful. The quest for profits is not enough to ensure getting them, and only the surplus value currently being produced to meet the expansion needs of already accumulated capital can produce profits; but the magnitude of this surplus value is an unknown quantity and is only indirectly expressed in the ups and downs of the business cycle.

The business cycle in the Western countries was, it is true, marred by inflation, but it also brought about an economic growth that in the public eye meant prosperity and aroused expectations of a continued and perhaps permanent boom. The accelerating inflation rate, however, was an unmistakable sign that to maintain the level of profitability needed to continue economic growth would require increased reliance on government expansion of money and credit, and that without these government measures, growth would slacken. Thus continued economic growth depended on state money and credit policies, and to clear the way for them, all the encumbrances that had been placed in its way by past developments had to be removed. The first measure to this

end, therefore, was the abolition of commodity money at the national level, later to be followed internationally by the abolition of the gold convertibility of the international reserve currency.

Production continued to decline and unemployment to increase, while inflation proceeded unabated, until it finally became evident that the crisis-prone nature of capitalist accumulation could not be eliminated by state manipulations of the economy. The growing inflation rate, which was but the outward reflection of a credit expansion based partly on the anticipation of future profits, was also unable to prevent the decline in real profits. Expansive monetary and credit policies only drove prices upward without notably increasing production. With profits falling, capitalists were reluctant to invest and resorted to price rises to recoup their losses. The monopolies' power to fix prices arbitrarily facilitated this process, which was already contained in embryo in money and credit policies. The growing inflation rate threatened to develop into a gallop ultimately as pernicious to a capitalist economy as was a state of crisis made worse by deflation. Inflation can, of course, be abolished by reversing monetary and credit policies — not so, however, the shortage of profits, which accelerates price inflation. Any restriction on the expansion of money and credit is reflected in a further decline in economic activity and in rising unemployment. Governments, therefore, are reluctant to effect a radical reversal in their money and credit policies. Since, however, the crisis is now a tangible reality despite the expansive money and credit policies, governments have a choice between two evils and take what appears to them the lesser of the two in the given circumstances. Brakes are applied to inflation by contracting credit and reducing the supply of money or by state price and wage regulations, although at a critical point the government will revert from deflationary measures back to an inflationary policy. Through applying alternative doses of deflation and inflation, efforts are made to arrest the inflationary process and at the same time prevent rapid economic disintegration, in the hopes that sooner or later profitability will improve and the economic recession will be brought to a halt.

The level of integration reached in the world economy ensures that the manifestations of crisis and boom take on international dimensions, although they may appear in one particular country first. The positive effect of the European and Japanese upswing on American capital expansion was reflected, for example, in the spread of multinational corporations, with their higher level of profitability. But every downturn also internationalizes, irrespective of its point of origin. In all the capitalist countries (and not only in the United States), profits over the last five years have been lower than at any other time in the postwar period, with systematic price rises being the means resorted to in attempts to prop them up or boost them. Once this process has been set in motion and further supported by government money and credit policies, prices soar cumulatively upward, affecting all capital entities alike. The result is not only rising prices on finished products but also a continuing revaluation of capital, the covering of higher production costs in advance by means of capital depreciations, the application of different inflation rates in calculations to secure profits, and overpricing to reduce the increased risk to business brought about by inflation.

The cause of accelerating inflation is not a supply that lags behind demand but a shortage of profits that drives prices up quite independently of supply and demand relations. Even where demand actually is lagging, prices do not fall but on the contrary adjust to this reduced demand by rising further. The need for expanding profits is so great that the supply may be reduced by contrived means, as, for example, was recently done by the international oil industry, which was able to boost its falling profits by holding back on production. Just as each individual capital entity within a country seeks ruthlessly to maintain and to enlarge its share in the contracting sum of social surplus value by pricing measures, at the international level this process assumes an even more blatant form, since the instruments of political power can also be used to supplement international competition. Thus among the first signs of a looming crisis is sharpened international competition, in which each country seeks with all the means at its disposal to secure or increase its share in world profits.

The cooling off of the postwar boom and the ineffectiveness, now becoming apparent, of the monetary and credit policies that had borne it along have brought about some extensive political changes within individual capitalist countries and on a world scale. The first measures taken were aimed at toning down competition by allaying imperialist antagonisms. One of the reasons for American opposition to the war in Indochina on the part of capital was undoubtedly the enormous public consumption, to which there seemed to be no limits and, moreover, no prospects of being off-set by real profits in the future. To some capitalists, at least, the growing public spending appeared to hamstring economic expansion and reduce their ability to compete internationally. The end of the war required at least a short-term accord with the rival powers in Southeast Asia. The imperialist contradictions between Russia and China, which also bore on Asia, provided the chance for America to withdraw on the basis of the status quo, and the imperialist solution to Asian power politics was put off until some future time. It was hoped that the pacification of the world situation would relieve at least some of the more threatening signs of crisis by enabling economic relations to expand — a view that the former adversaries in the cold war shared, despite their other differences.

In market theory the removal of political restrictions on world trade should bring at least a partial improvement in the economic situation and moreover, avert a catastrophic crash that could easily plunge a politically explosive world into a third world war. But a crisis that has its origins in production cannot be prevented by measures confined to the level of trade and commerce. Indeed, trade itself becomes an aggravating factor in the crisis when each nation is obliged to tend to its own special interests in opposition to those of other countries. So it happens that the removal of trade restrictions of one kind is attended by the creation of restrictions of another kind, e.g., tariff policies, import prohibitions, the breaking of regional and international agreements, and a growing chaos in all economic relations. The internationalization of economics which the boom had promoted is forced to reverse its course, and once again priority is given to national interests, as the world economy sinks into further disarray.

All the signs of a deepening crisis are currently at hand, but how far they will develop cannot be foretold. They could conceivably assume the catastrophic proportions of the last great crisis;

but it is more likely that the economy will go into a slow process of decline, since the state has not exhausted all its means of influencing it. If state measures are not sufficient to induce a new upswing, they are at any rate still capable of preventing a period of precipitous decline at the cost of the future of capitalism. There are limits, however, to how far this policy can go, and the scope of the crisis determines where exactly these limits lie.

Notes

1. Through the *Istituto per la Riconstruzione Industrielle* (IRI) the Italian government owns numerous financial and industrial enterprises, including Alfa Romeo, Alitalia, steel works, oil, telephone and telegraph, radio, television, and banks. IRI enterprises do not differ essentially from private enterprises. They partake of the general capital market. Shares can be bought and sold on the stock exchange.

2. The multiplier effect released through public works was mentioned by O. T. Mallery shortly before and after World War I. He pointed out that public works not only increase employment but that this increase, by creating additional buying power, leads to additional employment ("A National Policy; Public Works to Stabilize Employment," in *The Annals of the American Academy of Political and Social Science,* January 1919). Likewise David Friday, "Maintaining Productive Output: a Problem of Reconstruction," in *Journal of Political Economy,* January 1919. I. M. Clark investigated the role of the multiplier and published his results in *Economics of Planning Public Works,* 1935.

1974

2

Deflationary Inflation

It is popular nowadays to distinguish between the inflation of time past and a new kind of inflation, which accordingly requires a new explanation, although in its monetary aspects inflation has the same features now as before: rising prices or the diminishing buying power of money. While its opposite, deflation, was viewed as contracted demand resulting in falling prices, inflation was explained by insufficient supply, driving prices up. Since, however, in this view it is the commodity market that determines price formation, little attention was paid to monetary policy. Money was seen merely as a veil concealing real processes, obfuscating them but altering little in their essential nature.

This theory was also accompanied by the illusion, still lingering today, that the quantity of money in circulation in the economy has an important influence on commodity prices and that price stability depends on an equilibrium between the quantity of money and the total volume of goods. The modern advocates of the quantity theory of money also attribute deflation and inflation to a too slow or too rapid growth in the supply of money, and as a remedy to these anomalies they propose the creation of money adjusted proportionally to actual economic growth.

Thus in money theory the economic cycle is represented as an expansion and contraction of the money supply and of credit not commensurate with the real situation. But it was expected that the equilibrium mechanism of the market would ultimately steer things back to normal. The crisis of the thirties, however, which seemed to have taken hold for good, put an end once and for all to any notions of such an automatic self-establishing equilibrium. In Keynes's view, which dominated bourgeois economic theory in the years that followed, the laws of the market were no longer capable of bringing about economic equilibrium with full employment. A developed capitalist economy, claimed Keynes, made for a decline in effective demand and with it a fall-off in investments and growing unemployment. Although this theory was designed specifically to explain economic stagnation during the period between the two world wars, it was quickly given universal status and regarded as the last word in the science of economics; to avoid the deflationary state of the depression and to restore economic equilibrium with full employment, state measures were needed to stimulate overall demand.

Central manipulation of the amount of money in circulation and of the amount of credit was not sufficient for such purposes, claimed Keynes. Instead, fiscal means, e.g., deficit financing of public spending and adjustments in the exchange rates, were needed. The inflationary monetary and fiscal policies that such measures entailed would prove to be what was needed to beat the crisis. However, an inflationary course must not lead to a demand that exceeded what the production capacity could supply. It must come to a halt when full employment was achieved in a new price equilibrium.

Every capitalist crisis, no matter what its imputed causes, manifests itself in a declining accumulation of capital. The share of social production earmarked for expansion is considerably reduced or even fully eliminated, curtailing total social production in the process. Seen from the restricted view of the market, however, this process appears as overproduction of goods or insufficient demand. The depression that resulted was a deflationary process which affected both prices and production, but which at the same time brought about substantial changes in the economic structure and prepared the way for a new economic boom. The depression became an instrument for overcoming economic crisis, and although not deliberately encouraged, it was passively allowed to run its course.

Inflation implied the creation of money by the state, which impaired the price mechanism. This was seen as a violation of the laws of the market, caused not by factors inherent in the economic system but by an arbitrary monetary policy. Inflation was resorted to in order to finance wars beyond what was possible with tax revenue alone or in order to eliminate excess state debts and hence indebtedness in general. However, in economic crisis situations there had been a general reliance on the restorative effects of deflationary depression until the twentieth century.

As capital grew it created obstacles to its own further expansion. Its periodic crises became more and more oppressive and persisted long enough to create a real danger that the deflationary process would lead to social upheaval rather than to a new boom. To prevent this from happening, state economic interventions were in order in the great crisis that followed the 1929 crash; their theoretical justification came later. This interventionist policy sought to achieve by inflationary means what seemed no longer attainable by deflationary methods.

Following traditional theory, Keynes assumed that the interest rate was dependent on the quantity of money in circulation. An increase in the money supply would decrease the interest rate and spur new investments, which in turn would increase employment and raise prices and profits. Since the state had the power to create more money, it was a matter of government decision whether the way to economic recovery would be through lower interest rates. However, the profitability of capital had already fallen so far that even a reduction in interest rates would not be sufficient stimulus for new investments. It would therefore be necessary to make up for the defective private demand by creating more public demand. However, since an increase in public spending by way of taxation would cut even more into the profits of the private sector, it would have to be financed through state deficits.

Deficit financing would increase the amount of money in circulation without necessarily leading to inflation. The technique, of course, was not to print more money, which would depreciate the currency, but merely to expand state credit which would absorb idle private capital and finance the increased public demand. This added demand would, it was expected, stimulate the economy as a whole sufficiently to bring it out of the depression and into a boom, which in turn would enlarge the state's tax revenue to such a degree that it would be able to pay off its depression-incurred debts in a new period of prosperity.

In the light of bourgeois economic theory, and especially its theory of money, it seemed quite plausible that by increasing the money supply and public demand simultaneously, an interrupted process of accumulation might be set into motion again. The coordinated employment of monetary and fiscal policies would not only counteract the deflationary trend of the crisis, they would in addition initiate a new period of upswing, which although containing inflationary tendencies, need not degenerate into a real inflation as long as unused money and real capital were still available. The specter of inflation would loom only if a new disproportionality arose between the means of payment and commodity production. But this was a real possibility only when full employment was reached, and then it could be combated by state-initiated deflationary policies. In short, it was imagined that a theory and practical policy had finally been found which would place the economic cycle under conscious state control.

Bourgeois economics begins and ends with market relations, and hence it can only obliquely touch on the production processes underlying market events. These processes it sees as being determined by demand. In Keynes's theory it is a relatively declining demand for consumer goods that brings about a decreasing demand for capital goods. Under such conditions further investments can only reduce profits, and for that reason they are not made. The way back to full employment would require, first, improving the profit rate of private capital, and second, filling a chronic lack of investments by state-induced production. In the light of the experience of the great economic crisis, the second of these measures seemed to be a precondition for the first, although it was still not clear whether state-induced demand was a temporary or permanent necessity in a modern market economy. Keynes himself thought that the future of capitalist economy depended on increasing state control.

In the bourgeois conception the economy appears as a circular process in which total income must equal total expenditures. It was therefore immaterial what specifically went into total income and total expenditures. The social distribution of income is presumed to be determined by the various contributions of the

different factors of production to total production. Since, however, not all income is consumed, the cycle can only really be completed when the saved income is reinvested. The upshot is that
state-induced production, regardless of what ends it may serve, is
able to reduce or eliminate completely any discrepancy that may
arise between total income and total expenditures. But this requires that the state be given the power to dispose of the saved —
but not invested — capital. In its hands money capital that was not
being used to expand real capital could restore equilibrium to the
economic cycle.

With this conception the bourgeois world deprives itself of
any realistic insight into the economic process in general and into
the problem of inflation in particular. Just as it does not distinguish between social production as such and specific capitalist production, so too it does not distinguish between productive and unproductive capitalist production. Any kind of production for
which there is a demand on the market enjoys equal status as far
as it is concerned, and any kind of demand appearing on the market finds its match in production. It does not distinguish, therefore, between demand created by capitalist production for profit
and demand created by public spending. The latter, too, is a demand that private capital can meet with an adequate supply and
reap the profits accruing therefrom. The growing state debt aside,
the economy is revived by the increased public demand, which in
turn has a positive influence on private market demand. The growing amount of money in circulation and expanding income are balanced by an undifferentiated and expanding production on the expenditure side of the ledger, which could partly or wholly eliminate unemployment.

The only vulnerable point in this description of events was
the growing public debt; for this there is no equivalent in the production sphere, since the additional government demand consists
of goods and services that enter public consumption and therewith
impede the expansion of real capital in proportion to their magnitude. The mere expansion of production without a proportional
increase in profit is equivalent to a partial destruction of capital,
since some of the capital used ceases to be productive, i.e., ceases
to produce additional capital.

The inability, whether conscious or unconscious, of bourgeois economic theory to understand this point forces it to entertain the ungrounded and empirically unverifiable expectation that the acceleration principle, as it is called, and the multiplier effect of new investments can bring about the desired economic revival in which total production will grow more rapidly relative to state-induced production, so as ultimately to bring state-induced demand back down to its normal level. In any event, the growing public debt entailed no risks as long as total production increased more rapidly than did the public debt.

In contrast to the autonomous expansion of capital, however, state-induced expansion of total production is characterized by the fact that a portion of the profits on which it is based derives from public loans rather than from increased production.

If this kind of economic pump priming has become a necessity, it is still limited by the limitations of state credit. As state-induced production goes into public consumption, it cannot serve accumulation; and as the profits accruing to private capital from state loans are not newly created but merely represent already existing money capital, only the share of total profits obtained in the private sector is available for capital accumulation. Not only is the profit accruing to private capital from state-induced production a part of total production, but the share of total production that appears to generate this profit is also lost to capitalist accumulation by being allocated to public consumption.

Thus public spending means a growing public debt, which ultimately can only be financed and paid off by profit-creating capital. The profits of earlier production periods, which in the sterile form of money capital have lost their function as capital, are eaten up by state-induced production and appear to the entrepreneurs and creditors engaged in state-induced production as profits and interest. This process is both real and illusory. It is real for individual capitals but illusory from the standpoint of the social capital, since the profits that fall to the individual producer do not owe their existence to production itself but to the consumption of money capital placed at the disposal of the state. Thus in bourgeois theory the elimination of a state budget deficit is feasible only on the expectation of some future surplus, i.e., a prosperity that would allow the state debt to be paid off. This would require future profits that must not only be adequate to the further demands of accumulation but, in addition, large enough to replace the money capital used up in public consumption. If this capital is not replaced, it would mean that some capital had been expropriated by the state for public ends. From the standpoint of capital as a whole, this would mean that some existing capital had been swallowed up by the crisis, and state deficit financing would therefore have achieved the same result as capital destruction achieved by deflationary depressions in the past.

In contrast to deflationary depression, however, this process appears outwardly as expanding production. The more production expands, the more must the profitability of capital be backed up by state deficits, i.e., by more loans. But since idle money capital is a given finite magnitude, the process breaks down at the point where the state must be refused further loans. At this point the process could be continued only through an arbitrary proliferation of paper money, until it finally erupted into open inflation.

Deficit financing is also an inflationary process, although it can be held in check by the limitations imposed on the state debt. It is inflationary because the social profit corresponds to an increased production only apparently; in reality it is insufficient. Capital that lies idle because of insufficient profitability enters capital circulation through the monetary effects of the public debt, where it helps to expand production, but not profits, proportionately. In relation to the total capital, of which money capital is a part, the increased amount of money in circulation stands in contrast to a profit mass out of proportion to it, since a portion of accrued profits derives not from production but from a transfer of already existing capital to the profits column.

Since, however, capitalist economy is production for profit, which must be measured in terms of total capital and must be adequate to the needs of capital accumulation, for the individual capitals the discrepancy between expanded total production and the total profits actually produced manifests itself as a fall in the rate of profit, which, however, can be offset by commensurate price increases as long as production is expanding and competition is hence not as sharp. While neither profit nor interest accrues from state investments, as a part of total production, the individual capitals, participating in state-induced production, do yield both; this contradiction resolves itself, on the one hand, through a different redistribution of total profits among individual capitals, and on the other hand — insofar as the competitive averaging of rate of profit still asserts itself — through a fall in the general rate of profit, which then is offset by rising prices. The social costs of state-induced production are then distributed over the population at large in the form of price inflation.

The rise in commodity prices occurring hand in hand with expanding production is thus the capitalist response to the pressure put on the general rate of profit by state-induced demand. State intervention is, of course, itself a crisis phenomenon and would not occur were capital capable of expanding on its own. But like the crisis itself, this "crisis solution" is marked by the reduction of profits, although it manifests itself in rising, not falling, prices.

If an "excess" of capital unable to find profitable employment appears as a general shortage of money, and hence as deficient demand, then profits fall along with commodity prices. The fall in prices can be arrested and its course reversed by state interventions. In the past the approach was to reduce supply, i.e., use-values were not produced or were simply destroyed. However, since it is not supply and demand which, along with prices, determines the level of profits, these measures proved ineffective. The problem had to be tackled from the profit side.

At any price level enterprise profits represent the difference between costs and market prices. Every firm seeks to reduce costs to maintain its profits. The costs a firm can influence directly are the costs of wages: it may simply lower them, or it may try to improve the productivity of labor. The magnitude of the average rate of profit is determined by the total surplus value created by labor in relation to total capital. A crisis implies a decline in the general rate of profit, which for the time being renders the further growth of total capital inadmissible. Under such conditions every enterprise intensifies its efforts to maintain, and where possible to increase, its profits by reducing costs. This sharpens competition, which in turn further obstructs restoration of the required level of profitability and prolongs the depression and the destruction of capital. Nonetheless, even as capital as a whole is contracting, the strivings of individual capital entities bring about an expansion, if at a slower pace, of total surplus value. The larger mass of surplus value relative to the reduced value of total capital raises the rate of profit, and further accumulation becomes possible. Firms that cannot enlarge their profits stand on the brink of bankruptcy. On the other hand, surviving capital entities have a broader field over which to range. This process effectively amounts to the concentration of capital and is itself an instrument for expanding profits.

These so-called microeconomic changes have their repercussions at the macroeconomic level, and through the instrumentality of crisis they restore the profit rates needed for further capital accumulation. If this were not so, the crisis cycle would be incomprehensible. State interventions into the economy, on the other hand, are applied directly to the macroeconomic level, to find a shortcut to the slow-paced regulatory results of the microeconomic process. Their aim, too, is to increase profits, but they hope to achieve this through the circulation process. Keynes himself saw that to reduce wages by inflationary means was not only easier, it could also be accomplished more generally than if one had to rely on the independent action of numberless individual firms. A general price rise, along with a slower rise in wages, must increase profits so long as at the same time the general demand is also increased through deficit financing of public spending. Without this last measure, designed to blunt the edge of competition, the wage reductions might readily prove to be unsatisfactory and the economic pinch grow worse.

In order to inflate commodity prices under depression conditions, deficient demand, which appears as a shortage of money, must be eliminated. This is done by the creation of more money and by state credits that pump money already at hand back into circulation. This enhances nominal buying power, but increased profits through higher commodity prices will be possible on this account only if costs do not undergo an equivalent rise. Otherwise commodities (including labor power) would only be tagged with higher prices without the profitability of capital having been changed in the least. Since, however, not all commodity prices rise at a uniform rate, and moreover, it is extremely difficult if not impossible for the price of labor power to keep pace with the general price rises, price inflation ultimately results in an improvement in capitalist profitability.

Thus by means of an inflationary money and pricing policy, both production and income distribution are modified, because the ratio of wages to profits shifts in favor of the latter. This is controlled inflation when the determination and limitation of the amount of money in circulation is left to the discretion of the state. Controlled inflation, originally conceived as a means to get through a crisis, soon became, at least for economists, a precondition for economic growth as such. Even if a steady state of full employment were achieved, demand could be further expanded, they said, by a "dampened inflation," with the effect that debts would suffer a steady devaluation, thereby spurring investment.

The English economist Phillips undertook some statistical investigations in an attempt to demonstrate that a close empirical correlation existed between the employment level and inflation; the result of his efforts subsequently became one of the bulwarks of bourgeois economic theory under the name of the Phillips curve.[1] This curve shows that a rising level of employment was always accompanied by a rise in prices, while growing unemployment was accompanied by a price decline. Thus it seemed that full employment went hand in hand with inflation. Since the employment level depended on demand, it would follow that inflation was a consequence of rising demand, which drives prices, along with wages, upward. Demand-induced or wage inflation would rule out full employment with price stability, although it should allow the option between combating inflation by means of unemployment or combating unemployment by means of inflation.

Although the significance of these questionable statistical findings, for which no theory was ever offered in explanation, was disputed, they did, however, offer a demonstration, if a somewhat troubled one, of the efficacy of state economic controls. The goal was no longer economic equilibrium with price stability but the restoration of an "inflationary equilibrium," in which inflation rode the back of full employment. Still economists considered the social costs thereby incurred to be a small price to pay for a growing, full-employment economy, especially if inflation could be kept within socially optimum bounds by skillful manipulation of the labor market. It could not, however, be determined whether the wage increases that were so evident a part of prosperity were matched by price rises. But no statistical demonstration is needed to show that wages improve as the demand for labor increases. Wage increases, however, are kept within limits by the industrial reserve army, which never completely disappears, and by the need for adequate profitability — an indispensable condition for accumulation and hence for a rising demand for labor. The simple fact that capital accumulation will take place during a period of prosperity is proof in itself that capital has maintained its profitability despite rising wages.

An economic boom not only drives prices up, it also improves the productivity of labor, which actually should lower prices. According to bourgeois theory, under conditions of general competition, if production costs are reduced, prices, including the price of labor, should fall as well, without real wages necessarily being diminished in like measure. More consumer goods should mean lower prices, so that, although money wages should decline, buying power would remain intact. If wages did not decline, or if they declined more slowly than the general price level, this would be at the expense of other factors of production. But then economic equilibrium, supposedly sustained by the price mechanism, would be upset, and either wages would have to be forced downward or the prices of goods raised to restore it. In this view, therefore, price inflation is ultimately the result of a faulty wage policy.

But the illusion of a pricing mechanism kept in equilibrium by general competition was soon discarded, to be replaced in the bourgeois camp by theories of monopoly price fixing and state intervention. Yet monopolies themselves were held only partly to blame for monopolistic price formation, namely, where price fixing exceeded the average level of profit. But because monopolies were able to reap excess profits through price fixing, they could also afford to accept monopolistically fixed wages, which increased costs. In this way monopoly capital and monopolized labor worked together to drive prices up. Once this demand-, wage-, or cost-induced inflation had taken root, it would accelerate steadily unless it was arrested by state intervention. The answer to inflation was thus a price and wage policy that would restore stability.

State control of prices and wages could, at least in theory, curb inflation without thereby relieving the conditions that had led to inflation. For if capital is to have a free hand to expand itself, it must have sufficient profits. In a monopoly-dominated capitalist economy, capital accumulation must take place through the monopolies. Monopoly profits reflect the need for profits higher than those obtained under conditions of competition. Monopolies are the outgrowth of progressive concentration and centralization of capital through competition, but neither they nor competition can alter the given mass of profit. Neither form of competition, monopoly or pure, does more than distribute total social profit. A price and wage policy that made monopolistic profit impossible would also undermine capital accumulation.

Monopoly profits come from circulation, not from production. Of course, capitalist excess profits come from processes in the production sphere as well, when there is an above-average rise in labor productivity; the reduced costs then enable firms to earn higher than average profits on their products. But this form of excess profits is only temporary and disappears again when the improved production methods become more general. Monopoly profit differs from this form of continually vanishing and reappearing excess profit in that under monopoly, competition has been largely abolished. A monopoly profit rate is achieved through control of prices. In order, however, for profits to multiply of themselves, the production relations between values and surplus value must shift in favor of the latter. Profits must be produced, and it is only those profits actually *produced* that determine capital accumulation and, accordingly, the state of the economy in general.

If the progressive monopolization of capital is a reflection of and response to the increasing profit difficulties of accumulation, it is clear that the partial elimination of competition can hardly be expected to increase social profit. Monopoly profits are created at the expense of individual capitals still caught up in competition, which forces them also to raise prices to avoid losses. Thus *all prices* become in a sense more or less monopoly prices, although the degree to which this is so will vary widely, which indeed provides the whole process with some "sense": namely, the reapportionment that it effects in social production in favor of capital expansion. Nor is any of this contradicted by the observation, often heard, that monopolies impede rather than promote capital accumulation, as supposedly evidenced by all the idle production capacity. But this argument says no more than that during periods of economic stagnation, monopolies strive to keep themselves alive at the expense of weaker capital entities and at the expense of the population at large. To reproduce itself as capital, monopoly capital must also accumulate; and it therefore endeavors, through a monopolistic price policy, to effect a further division of profit and wages in circulation to add to the primary separation between wages and profit in the production process.

Monopoly prices are just as necessary to capital as competitive prices before them, even if they are fixed by monopolies in accordance with their special needs. The concentration of profit in the hands of the monopolies by way of price policies is in the final analysis a concentration of capital. As competition progressively declines, however, this source of monopoly profit dwindles, and the profit rate of monopoly capital becomes the average rate of profit. At this point monopoly price manipulation would rest alone on the relation between wages and profit and could just as well be replaced by administrative controls.

Although monopoly price formation must, like capital accumulation, arrive at a dead end, it has at first some positive effects. Like the spurious profits generated by production induced by public spending, monopoly profits stimulate the economy precisely because they are obtained by the roundabout way of price inflation. Thus, on the one hand, we have state-induced production, and on the other, the need to promote capital accumulation by way of further monopolization: in either case the result is inflation.

After World War II bourgeois economics deluded itself that it not only had discovered the secret of crisis, but also that it possessed the means to nip any further crisis in the bud; the expansion of capital, therefore, which was taking place largely on its own momentum, certainly was not designed to undermine the conviction that any economic recession could be countermanded with the proven anticyclical measures. This conviction persisted until the advent of deflationary inflation, where growing unemployment was accompanied by an accelerating rate of inflation. The first response to this situation was almost automatic: the Keynesian tactic of a wage freeze. Together with high interest rates, this freeze artificially maintained prices, reduced the profitability of capital, and hindered its expansion. The frozen wages of depression stood in contrast to the rising wages of the "full-employment" period, which were blamed for the "wage-price spiral." It had, indeed, been acknowledged for some time that full employment could have inflationary effects, but they were, it was argued, the signs of prosperity and should be seen in a positive light. That things had actually developed differently was due not to the system itself but to factors stemming from outside it, namely, the irrational mania of the workers to get more out of the system than was in it.

This understandable and widespread nonsense,[2] which of course from the viewpoint of capital makes quite good sense, would not even be worthy of special comment were it not often encountered in supposedly "leftist" explanations of the crisis.[3] Under conditions of full employment, whether brought about by the autonomous movement of capital or by state-induced production, or both simultaneously, it is obviously more difficult to cut back wages or prevent their rise. It is also clear that the organized workers are able to improve their wages through economic struggles. Finally, it is evident that under such conditions capitalists seek in some cases to avoid conflicts by granting pay raises, which they can then recoup by raising prices correspondingly. Nor is there need to dispute that the successes of organized labor in this domain also often enable unorganized workers to improve their situation as well: in a period of boom wages are generally able to follow prices upward.

But in a period of recession profits decline. If wages do not fall in pace with profits, the depression deepens. To get out of depression it is not enough to bring the fall in wages in line with the fall in profits; profits must be augmented at the expense of wages. In the past in crisis situations, the heightened competition among workers for jobs led to a reduction in wages. The institutionalization and monopolization of economic labor organizations, it is claimed, has now made this impossible. For the bourgeoisie even the defense of existing wage levels is sufficient to explain both crisis and inflation.

It is quite possible, and indeed undoubtedly also often the case, that a wage policy favorable to capital cannot be put through. In any event, bourgeois statisticians have no difficulty proving that both money wages and real wages increased and often exceeded the increase in productivity. But other statistics exist as well showing that what workers gain in wages is taken from them again later in the circulation process.[4] Whatever else such statistics may mean, they are no acceptable empirical demonstration that inflation is due to wages, or that the opposite is the case. First, price relations tell us nothing about the value and surplus value relations underlying them; yet in the end they determine the state of the economy. Second, profits may actually be higher when wages are also up than when they are low, if the share of surplus value in the total value of production is sufficiently large. Indeed, this surplus value rests not only on the extremely limited, statistically discernible increase in labor productivity; it also depends on the total surplus value produced on a world scale in proportion to world capital as total capital, and for this there are no statistics available. Even apart from these considerations, however, the very existence of an economic boom demonstrates that however wages go, profits increase more rapidly than the share of labor in the social product. True, the postwar boom was accompanied by creeping, though uneven, inflation[5] from the very outset. But the reason for this lay not with rising wages, which went beyond the increase in labor productivity, but with the fact that the boom and its continued existence were possible only because of inflationary price policies, which, moreover, had over a relatively long period of time been used liberally and effectively to maintain the wage-profit relation necessary for economic expansion. But why has this accumulation period, in contrast to earlier booms, been so consistently inflationary? In the economic cycles of the past century, every crisis was preceded by the inflationary phenomena of a heated up economy. Wages, prices, and interest rates rose. A wide expansion of credit concealed a decline in profitability that had already begun, thereby delaying the end of the boom. Ultimately the expectations the boom had created would prove false. Profit remained behind production, and expansion finally ground to a halt.

The expansion of private credit sets its own limits through the rising interest rates it inevitably brings with it, but even without this it must cease as profits continue to decline. Depression is the outgrowth of boom, but if it is to be avoided — and that, after all, was the purpose of state interventions — the contraction of private credit must be made up for by the expansion of state credit activities. But such measures do not increase the total mass of profits, and the result is a situation resembling a credit-sustained but already unprofitable phase of the boom, except that state credits are not limited in the same way as are private credits.

In other words, capital now "accumulates," though profits are inadequate, without this at first being evident owing to the mechanism of the state debt. There is no direct pressure to reduce wages, since the profitability of capital can remain at a steady level even as wages rise as long as demand is sufficiently inflated by state-induced production.

If capital were unable to increase its profitability on its own, the state-induced upswing would soon have to come to an end. An autonomous expansion of profit, however, is possible only by way of an increase in labor productivity, i.e., a higher rate of exploitation of labor, which relatively depreciates labor's value. As this is difficult to achieve under full-employment conditions, capital attempts to obtain the profits it requires for accumulation by way of price formation. The result is the same: a growing share of total production falls to capital, while proportionately less goes to the work force.

Not only does the relationship between wages and profits change, the distribution of the social product generally shifts in favor of capital accumulation. The social layers with fixed incomes, which find it difficult, if not impossible, to adjust to the inflationary trend, must give up more of their income to capital. The savings of the "little man" are eaten up progressively as the value of productive capital rises in pace with inflation. It was this process of creeping inflation which contained the secret of prosperity. The disadvantages of inflation seemed for the time being to be offset by the advantages of economic boom.

Although the dependence of capitalist prosperity on capital accumulation is immanent to the system, it is not recognized by bourgeois economic theory. For bourgeois economists inflation is caused by a demand in excess of production, or even by the immoderate claims of the workers, although the very universality of inflation is a patent contradiction of this view; indeed, inflation plagues even countries with extremely low wages, where there is no monopoly of labor and where demand lags far behind supply. Inflation occurs in depressions, where one would expect deflation. The international character of inflation is proof enough that inflation involves more than merely the erratic consequences of high wages in a few countries.

Now, however, when inflation and crisis exist side by side in the leading capitalist countries, the contention that inflation is a consequence of full employment and demand outstripping supply is no longer tenable. The only thing left to blame, therefore, is high wages. And despite all the monopolization of labor, or perhaps even because of it, the bourgeoisie still finds rising unemployment a good taskmaster. Wage contracts, often long term, have with a few unimportant exceptions made it impossible to counteract the burden of steeply rising prices or to make up for past omissions through wildcat strikes; all the more reason, therefore, to take advantage of the all-pervasive depression to reap inflationary profits. One must, so one hears in quite a number of trade unions, face the facts: inflation eats away at any wage rise, making continued demands meaningless. What is now necessary to get out of the depression is a responsible wage policy, i.e., capital must be given the chance to regain its lost profitability.[6]

It is of course clear that if wages are down, prices can be reduced; but although possible, this need not become a reality. Prices depend on other things besides "market relations" and "factor costs," e.g., indirect taxes, subsidies, stabilization programs, and monopolistic manipulations. Even where production is steadily declining, where there is mass unemployment, and where wages are at starvation levels, prices can still continue to climb into the blue beyond; and indeed in the past they have done so, with the ultimate result that inflation degenerates into hyperinflation. Even before inflation gets out of control, depression, which drives wage costs down, is not sufficient to put an end to rising prices. In any event the most recent anti-inflationary policies have had very disappointing results, which moreover are all the more questionable in that they have led to situations compelling a recourse to inflation to keep the social fabric intact.

State deflationary or inflationary policies are not measures to control the economy so much as government reactions to processes that are already beyond control. The real development of capital is determined by the law of value, i.e., capital profitability and capital accumulation. State interventions are aimed merely at superficial market phenomena whose root causes are to be found in the production sphere, that is, in production relations. State reactions are therefore just as blind as these processes themselves; if they coincide at all with the events underlying developments on the market, it is by pure chance.

State interventions may fail to measure up to expectations, or they may lead even to adverse results. Whatever the case, the theories associated with them are discredited and therefore lose their ideological function. With no explanation for the present inflation forthcoming, the only thing left in store is a regression to an earlier standpoint, already abandoned once: namely, the empty hope that the equilibrium mechanisms of the market will turn out after all to have some clout left in them. Specifically, it is now asserted by some that all state intervention into the economy should be rejected, with perhaps the exception of "correct" monetary policy, such as advocated by Milton Friedman, and to opt, once again, for a "cure" by way of depression in order to reach a new boom. It is said

> The idea that the prevailing inflation finds no explanation in economic theory is pure nihilism. Likewise, the idea that it cannot be ended. All that is here required is a consistent monetary and fiscal policy, which curtails for a considerable length of time economic activity. Here of course lies the difficulty, namely, the necessary political determination. The responsible authorities have to make up their minds as to whether or not the majority of the population is ready to make the required sacrifices.[7]

Thus all the old disproven and discredited theories are revived to explain inflation and are expected to provide the key to its solution. The facts of the present inflation must be completely overlooked in the process, however; this inflation, like each of its predecessors, is no accident but the result of a quite definite economic policy. Inflation must be created, even if under the pressure of economic and political processes that originate not in conscious acts but from a compulsive need to accumulate capital.

World War I destroyed the customary world market relations as well as the relations among the national currencies, which were based on the gold standard. Under the gold standard fluctuations in the value of each individual currency were held within very narrow limits. If a nation elected to adopt inflationary means to combat an economic downturn, it had to free itself from these restrictions. Once the gold standard was abandoned, a monetary policy relatively independent of the world market could be adopted. But inflation remained withal a national affair that could be dealt with or not by individual governments as they saw fit. The different nations have thus tried to solve their profit problems in different ways, and inflation acquired a distinctly international character only after World War II.

World War II put a temporary end to capital accumulation. Half of international production was production for public consumption, which devoured both men and materials. Profits were written as state debts. To avoid an inflationary surge, rationing and forced saving were the policies adopted, although the rigor with which such measures were applied varied from one belligerent country to another. At war's end the world was not only a different place, it was totally impoverished. Only the United States, which was the least touched by the ravages of war and which even before the war had already assumed the number one position among the world's capitalist powers, was able to resume the accumulation process on the basis of an essentially unchanged capital structure. The other industrial countries had to resume again from a much lower level and had to go through a long period of accelerated accumulation before they once again regained their ability to compete. The restoration of the world market and of currency convertibility forced a series of currency reforms, often quite radical, and the Bretton Woods agreements, concluded while the war was still in progress, introduced a modified gold standard.

The postwar period witnessed a growing internationalization of capitalist production, which picked up steam rapidly and stimulated world trade. The autarchic tendencies of the prewar period, when each country endeavored to find a way out of its own problems at the expense of others, even to the point of imperialist wars of conquest, came to a temporary end in postwar events when the United States assumed hegemony over the world market. The "free world market'" was reborn out of the expanding American economy, helped along by the Marshall Plan and the export of private capital. Capital that could not be invested with adequate profitability in the United States itself found better conditions for value expansion in the nations engaged in reconstruction.

Until August 15, 1971, the international monetary system was based on the dollar, which was itself linked to a fixed price for gold, and the parities of other currencies were based on it. With other currencies tied firmly to the dollar and the dollar a reserve currency, the United States could settle its international payments obligations by expanding the dollar reserves of other countries. As long as the dollar's gold backing was felt to be secure, the export of dollars stimulated the world economy. Although the Americans acquired whole industries and national concerns developed into multinationals, these corporations were not only tolerated, they were even coveted as a means to get the European economy moving again. Between 1950 and 1970 direct U.S. investments increased tenfold, and in value terms the output of the multinational corporations exceeded total American exports by more than three times. This was part of the process that, together with the high accumulation rates attained in Europe, produced the long period of Western prosperity.

Since U.S. production made up approximately half of the total production of the capitalist world, changes taking place in its domestic economy were bound to make themselves felt throughout the rest of the world. To attain profit rates adequate to the needs of further accumulation, the share of American capital in total world production and in world trade had to be enlarged. This, of course, was true of all capitalist countries. At issue was how the surplus value produced worldwide was to be divided up. The postwar situation offered American capital a special opportunity to increase its share in world profits and at the same time put the devastated world economy back on its feet.

The war had also created new state capitalist countries that were very difficult to bring into the "free market economy" and in any case were anything but conducive to the expansion of private capital; hand in hand with the restoration of Western capital, therefore, went the attempt to contain the expansion of state-capitalist countries. The postwar period evolved in the atmosphere of the cold war, inaugurated by the first test of power, the Korean War, whose outcome remained indecisive.

The cold war laid claim to a large portion of public consumption. State debt, which had already grown to extreme proportions, grew further, if now more slowly and within narrower limits, and placed the profitability of capital under pressure. Originating in the United States, inflation pursued its onward course, until it finally embraced the entire world. It is impossible to say whether the postwar boom was responsible for the full, or near-full, employment achieved in the different countries, or to what extent this had continued to be dependent on state-induced production. In the United States, in any event, production capacity was never fully utilized at any time throughout this entire period, and unemployment stabilized at around 4 percent of wage earners. Worldwide, however, private capital expanded rapidly thanks to the rapid increase in labor productivity, an accelerating capital concentration worldwide, and an inflationary price policy.

However, one element contributing to the economic boom, the accompanying inflation, also revealed an inner weakness behind the outward prosperity, a weakness, moreover, that also emerged in the fact that this prosperity did not take hold in equal measure in all countries. It is of no importance, if it can be ascertained at all, whether it was the extremely high costs of imperialist policy which put the accumulation rate in the United States behind that in the other expanding countries, or whether this would have occurred in any event. However it may be, it is useless even to pose such a question, since imperialism cannot be separated from nationally organized capital. Since, however, public consumption always detracts from accumulation, the continuation of vast public spending necessitated by imperialist policy only made inflation worse.

How true this is becomes evident when we note how the average rate of inflation has accelerated since 1965. Because the American economy was already relatively stagnant, the only means of financing the costly war in Indochina and the ever growing demands of an imperialist world policy was more deficits and hence more inflation. As long as exchange rates were fixed, the growing inflation rate had to extend itself to other countries. The American balance-of-payments deficit continued to grow, enlarging the dollar reserves of other countries, and with it came more inflation.

Since a U.S. deficit meant a surplus for other countries, they initially felt no pressing concern to counter the accompanying inflationary tendencies, although American deficits in large measure meant a reduction in American, and hence in world profits. The growing dollar reserves of European countries helped to finance the American deficit, which meant an internationally accelerating inflation rate, but also a steady depreciation of monetary reserves. Under these conditions international competition, which also is fought out by way of monetary policies, could affect the diverse inflation rates, but not inflation itself.

For a capitalist economy the ideal state would be simultaneous domestic and external equilibrium, with stable prices and an even balance of payments. Keynes's theory essentially retained this ideal picture, except that it proposed to achieve this equilibrium through state interventions. While, however, domestic equilibrium is dependent on national monetary and fiscal policies, the external equilibrium of all countries would depend on the national monetary and fiscal policies of the United States as long as the world monetary system was based on the dollar with fixed currency exchange rates. Of course, this meant that the economic independence of every other country was largely undermined. Attempts to check inflation domestically would be at the price of impairing a nation's capacity to compete at the international level and hence could not be very extensively undertaken. Thus economic control at the national level was greatly impaired by the capitalist integration on the international scale.

As a worldwide phenomenon inflation was evidently a product of the accumulation difficulties due to the peculiarities of capitalist postwar expansion. The inflationary course concealed these difficulties, but it did not eliminate them; and although it was largely caused by the specific situation in the United States and was further tied in with the dollar's status as an international reserve currency, the breakdown of the Bretton Woods system and the return to free or floating exchange rates has demonstrated that there was more to inflation than the disintegrating effect of an international monetary system made obsolete by the growth of the world economy. Indeed, the system of flexible exchange rates has had no effect at all on the inflationary course.

The worldwide economic integration of national economies, and particularly of their capital markets, internationalized capital movements and price relations. World trade and the creation of international capitalist corporations made inflation a worldwide phenomenon. The increase in surplus value by way of inflation is facilitated by state monetary policy without being directly determined by it. No simple and obvious relationship exists between a country's monetary policy and that policy's economic repercussions, which may be modified extensively by relatively independent, autonomously unfolding economic processes. Once inflation gets started, however, it continues its course in relative independence of anything governments may consider doing, not only by way of price rises, which accelerate it further, but also by means of the greater involvement of international capital markets, the creation of additional sources of money and credit — such as the Eurodollar market — or even by the simple expansion of commercial credits. In this way inflation disguises itself as a shortage of investment capital, an insufficient liquidity, which seemingly cannot be satiated despite the inflationary increase in the money supply.

The large capital concerns still try to increase their share in total world profits by acquiring direct control of major shares of world production in addition to the profits they secure for themselves by the inflationary route. Such procedures are no more than capital concentration by way of international competition. In the process, however, capital markets are also internationalized, which means that they are no longer under any government's control. For instance, government restrictions on the export of capital to firm up the American payments balance were largely ignored because capital could be gained in the Euromoney and Eurocredit markets.

The Eurodollar market arose initially from the activities of U.S. banks outside of the United States. Over the last ten years their deposits abroad have grown from $10 to $185 billion. Other currencies were also traded, but the dollar predominated, representing 70 percent of total deposits. Apart from private credit transactions, the central banks of a number of countries also invest excess or unwanted reserves in the Eurodollar market or borrow from it to bridge over payments difficulties. The Eurodollar is preferred because it is under no government controls and operates with no reserve regulations, and hence can offer better terms to both borrower and lender.

Although significantly smaller than the American capital market, the Eurodollar market is still larger than the capital markets of other countries and is therefore able to avoid or find ways around government monetary and credit policies. Since it consists mainly of dollar deposits, there is of course a close correlation between the creation of money in the United States and the expansion of Eurodollars. While in the national banking systems the extent of the multiplier effect of any additional supply of money is twofold or threefold at most because of reserve regulations, the Eurodollar is under no such restrictions. The multiplier effect of the Eurodollar thus permits a much broader expansion of credit and contributes further to the purely speculative character of capital movements, as well as to the inflationary trend.

With inflation the price of money also rises. Since interest rates, however, are dependent on the rate of profit, they are able to contribute to inflation only slightly. Higher interest rates are not a sign that money has become dearer; rather they indicate that money has depreciated in value. The real interest rates usually remain unchanged, augmented only by the existing and expected inflation rates due to general price rises. Nonetheless even relatively stable interest rates are a burden for capital when profits are declining. Committed capital, which does not have the power to set prices monopolistically, can also find a steady interest rate intolerable. Thus under both inflationary and deflationary depression, bankruptcies multiply.

The cost of credit, whether high or low, should not be ascribed too much significance. Interest rates, which are included in capital production costs, constitute only a small percentage of total costs. In addition firms have long financed their own capital formation from their own proceeds. This presumably cuts into dividends, but it only means that a larger share of the accrued profits is used for accumulation purposes while a correspondingly smaller share goes to capitalist consumption. This tells us nothing about the absolute size of either of these shares, which, if profits are sufficient, may both increase together. If profits are inadequate, both can also be amassed by means of increased prices, whereby "internal financing" becomes a form of accumulation by means of inflation.

But it is not genuine accumulation. As this type of "self-financing" expands, the ability of other capitals to accumulate is correspondingly impaired. The total mass of profit available to the capitalist world economy remains where it is. Capital self-financing, like capital monopolization, implies then no more than a redistribution of total profits by way of price manipulations. Although high rates of profit may be achieved by means of arbitrary pricing policies, they imply an increasing rate of inflation, which sooner or later will also affect the privileged capital unfavorably. This does not mean that inflation stops, but only that henceforth it will not be a direct aid in expanding the privileged capitals. It will, at best, serve the maintenance of their profits under conditions of stagnation and decline.

Competition destroys capital, but it also improves the profitability of the capital that comes out on top in the struggle. Yet this does not mean that total social profits have grown in any significant measure — that is only possible through an increase in surplus value. Surplus value, however, can grow in only two ways: through an increase in the rate of exploitation, and by increasing the number of workers. But these two ways proceed along parallel courses only under certain conditions; their inherent tendency is to develop in opposing directions. Greater exploitation means that more products are produced with less expenditure of labor, i.e., there is an increase in the productivity of labor achieved through improved means of production and better methods of capitalist accumulation. Under these conditions the absolute number of workers may increase as well, but their number relative to accumulating capital decreases. Since surplus value is really only surplus labor, surplus value also decreases relative to the increase in capital and leads to a tendential decline in the rate of profit and the reduction of the pace of capital accumulation.

Under capitalism nothing in this situation can be changed, no matter how many other modifications are made elsewhere in the system. Like any previous boom, the most recent one also contained the seeds of its own decline. But whereas previously the decline was due mainly to a decrease in the mass of surplus value relative to the accumulated total capital, in the present period labor productivity in the industrial countries has increased to such an extent as to increase the costs of circulation disproportionately to production, and thus to accelerate the reduction of the rate of profit. Since production cannot be separated from distribution, only the total reproduction process of capital can tell us anything about its actual profitability. But in the past the proportion of workers engaged in production relative to those employed in circulation was more favorable to profit than it is today. As productivity in the production sphere has increased vastly, the number of workers employed in production has declined, while the number of those employed in distribution has risen disproportionately. But because so far it has not been possible to increase labor productivity in circulation to the same extent as in production, the tendential decline in the profit rate accompanying capital expansion has accelerated. The shift from capitalist productive labor to capitalist unproductive labor has been an important factor in the inflationary process.

With the steadily growing pressure on the profit rate, due to a variety of causes, the postwar expansion had to come to a halt despite all its inflationary props. The high profits that had been amassed down to the very last have turned out to be largely phantom profits deriving more from inflation than from production. Over the last two years, for instance, the high profits of many American firms have consisted of "inventory profits," i.e., profits stemming from the difference arising between the previous lower costs of the materials used in production and the current price of the finished product, which effects the present price of the materials used. According to U.S. Department of Commerce statistics, these "inventory profits" reached more than $37 billion in 1974, or 60 percent of the total profit increment.[8] But this process is nonrepeating unless the rate of inflation increases steadily, and even then it is so only for goods that require quite long production times. But whatever the case, the rate of accumulation is the true indicator of profitability, and in its terms even the high profits turn out to be inadequate.

Inflation has no future; during an economic upswing it can add fuel to the process, but it must be kept within certain limits if the profits it makes possible are not to vanish again into thin air. If an accelerating inflation rate gets out of control, its "positive" effect turns into its opposite. The chaos so characteristic of capitalism then becomes even more chaotic; internationally this shows up as recurrent monetary crises, with a resulting disintegration of world trade. Although the average annual world inflation rate was recently estimated at 12 percent, it affects each country quite differently depending on its competitive position on the world market. Persistent fluctuations in national currencies, said to make the squaring of international payments balances easier, miscarry, not only on the world market but also with regard to the continuing erosion of the national economies. The allegedly anti-inflationary Special Drawing Rights (SDR) of the International Monetary Fund, were designed to remedy a purported lack of liquidity; they were a system for squaring payments balances by means of uncovered mutual obligations; but it also proved to be merely one more inflationary measure, just like the dollar after its gold convertibility was abolished. As international economic relations become more and more difficult to see through and defy attempts to calculate business activity, capital is flowing across borders on a colossal scale in an attempt to glean profits from the monetary chaos and the particular difficulties of each country, insofar as they are not attainable by any other means.

Even under the best conditions, a steadily rising inflation rate leads eventually to economic stagnation. Inflation must then be halted at the point where it begins to have a negative effect on the economy. Just as governments add steam to inflation by their monetary and fiscal policies, contrary measures can slow its course. However, it is not within the power of governments to bring inflation totally to heel, since price inflation will continue despite deflationary government measures. This being the case, depression is aggravated in two directions: on the one hand, because of a stepped up general economic decline, and on the other, because of the multiplying social conflicts generated by the inflationary distribution of income.

Depression, like an upswing, sets limits to inflation. But any limit can be overstepped if one is willing to accept or is unable to avoid the attendant social risks; the hyperinflations of the past are ample testimony to this. But the risk is far greater when inflation is worldwide than when it is isolated within individual countries, as has been the case in the past. The bourgeoisie therefore tries to check it, but it can only do so by accepting lower profits, reducing public spending, and allowing depression to deepen. In 1974, for instance, total U.S. production fell by 10.4 percent, utilization of production capacity fell to 68 percent, and the official unemployment rate was 8.7 percent.

The economic situation of the last five years, which has been less serious, still required a 50 percent increase in public spending and budgetary deficits in excess of $100 billion. Without this public spending the economic decline would probably have been more considerable. As the depression spreads, the only way remaining to counteract its political consequences will be new state loans, which are even now beginning to dominate the capital market. Deficits of $125 billion for 1975 and 1976 are being considered, which will inevitably expand the money supply further. As the hopes that the depression will have a deflationary effect fade, they are replaced by prospects of a new boom contrived by inflationary means. Where all this will lead cannot be forecast with certainty, but at least one thing is sure: the present crisis, with its peculiar deflationary inflation, will keep the world in a perpetual state of unrest that could easily lead to catastrophe.

Notes

1. A. N. Phillips, "The Relation between Unemployment and the Rate

of Change of Money Wages in the United Kingdom, 1862-1957," in *Economica,* vol. 25, no. 100, December 1958, pp. 283-99.

2. From the extensive literature on this topic, see John Hicks, *The Crisis in Keynesian Economics,* Oxford, 1974, especially the chapter "Wages and Inflation"; also, Aubrey Jones, *The New Inflation,* Harmondsworth, 1973.

3. Z. B. A. Glyn and B. Sutcliffe, *British Capitalism, Workers and the Profit Squeeze,* London, 1972.

4. According to D. Jackson, H. A. Turner, and F. Wilkinson (see *Do Trade Unions Cause Inflation?,* Cambridge University Press, 1972), the total income of American workers in money wages rose by 4.7 percent annually between 1966 and 1970. The increase reduced to 0.8 percent in real income terms, and after tax deductions there turned out to be an annual decrease of 0.3 percent. In August 1974 A. F. Burns, Director of the U.S. Federal Reserve Board, observed that "over the last year the real income of workers in the United States fell by 5 percent" (*The New York Times,* August 16, 1974).

5. "From 1950 to 1960 the annual depreciation of money was 2.1 percent in the United States, 3.9 percent in England, 2.1 percent in Germany, 5.4 percent in France, 10.8 percent in Israel, 17.6 percent in Brazil, 36.6 percent in Bolivia, etc. There was no country whose money did not depreciate, although the rate of inflation varied widely from country to country" (First National City Bank, *Monthly Economic Letter,* New York, July 1974.

6. In this capital once again finds grounds for a cautious optimism, e.g., in the view of Ernst Wolf Mommsen, chairman of the board of F. Krupp GmbH, who states, "[since] now all those concerned, in particular the trade unions and corporations, have learned the lesson of the past two or three years, it would be wrong to keep putting through new nominal raises in prices and wages and to act as if alongside these nominal rises real rises are still possible in previous measures. The new wage statistics in the Federal Republic are a responsible step in the direction of keeping the nation's economy healthy and sound. The readiness of the trade unions to act, and finally after three years of stagnation to restimulate the investment capacity of German industry, must be evaluated positively. This has strengthened the willingness of German industry to invest and improve again our job security" (*Frankfurter Allgemeine Zeitung,* April 14, 1975).

7. *Monthly Economic Letter,* New York, First National City Bank, July 1974, p. 3.

8. *New York Times,* August 4, 1974.

1976

3

The Destruction of Money

Money as a means of exchange and as a hoard of wealth appears in many forms; as such it is as old as commerce itself and is encountered in the most diverse kinds of societies. Under capitalism, in addition to these general functions, it also exercises the specific function of embodying the social relations of production. In capitalist commodity production the commodity of labor power is exchanged for money. The purchaser of this special commodity uses it to enlarge his capital, measured in money terms. The primary aim of production is, accordingly, not the creation of goods for use; rather, it is only a means, albeit an indispensable one, for transforming a given quantity of capital into a larger quantity. Production of this sort is possible because labor power, as a commodity, has the ability to produce more than capitalists must pay for it; the basis of production, then, is the social relation between wage labor and capital.

In the circulation process capital alternately assumes commodity form and money form as it accumulates. Commodities and means of production may be transformed into money and vice versa, so that possession of capital is expressed as possession of money. Therefore money must itself be a commodity and be comparable in value terms with other commodities. In commodity exchange based on capitalist property relations, the division of social production into paid and unpaid labor assumes the character of value relations expressed in money terms. Although profit derives from unpaid labor time expended in production, to the capitalist it appears as a gain won in the market; indeed, the profit acquired from production must pass through the market in order to be realized. A commodity must first be transformed into money in order to enter into production or consumption as an item of use. It is money that gives production based on private property whatever social character it has.

Since capital expansion determines the course of social production, if the latter is to proceed smoothly it must be profitable enough to permit accumulation. If the rate of profit is insufficient, the accumulation rate falls; on the market the effect of this is a deficient effective demand and shortage of money. Although these phenomena are but symptomatic of difficulties in actual production, they are real enough at the market level, and every economic crisis will appear as a market and a money problem at the same time.

Since the relations of production admit of no alteration, bourgeois economics cannot think beyond pure market and money relations. Bourgeois monetary theory, however, has undergone some changes in the course of capitalist development. In classical political economy and in Marx's theory of value and surplus value, the value of money, like that of any other commodity, was determined by the average amount of labor time socially necessary to produce it. The value of money, in the form of gold or silver, was determined by the cost of producing it, and money itself served as the equivalent for all other commodities. Although through market competition commodity values take on the form of production prices, i.e., capitalist cost prices plus the average social profit, a commodity's value in terms of the labor time required to produce it still remains, since the average rate of profit is determined by the size of surplus value in relation to the total value of all commodities produced. Thus price does not abolish the value nature of commodities or the equivalent form of money.

With the emergence of the subjective theory of value, which ultimately ended in a hypostatization of prices, the bourgeois theory of value cut itself loose from all its former ties with classical monetary theory. Clearly the theory of marginal utility is inapplicable to the exchange value of money, since it cannot be determined by the subjective needs of consumers, as can the exchange value of other commodities, but is in fact juxtaposed to these needs as an already given objective value. There have been attempts, most notably by Ludwig von Mises,[1] to give the objective exchange value of money a subjective foundation by assuming that whatever the objective exchange value of money at the given moment, it always rested on prior subjective evaluations, which may be verified by tracing the development of money historically back to moneyless barter. But the derivation of money from a moneyless economy convinced few, and the attempt to define the value of money subjectively was given up.

It was not long until the entire theory of marginal utility was abandoned, since it obviously rested on circular reasoning. Although it tried to explain prices, prices were necessary to explain marginal utility. It was then decided that economic analysis did not need a special theory of value after all and could restrict itself wholly to the empirical magnitudes of money and prices. It would suffice, so it was claimed, to transform "marginal utility," with its psychological underpinnings, into a logic of choices or marginal analysis to reduce all market relations to an all-embracing common denominator. Just as every individual presumably ordered his income and expenditures rationally by means of marginal calculations so as to achieve the greatest measure of satisfaction of his needs, so the universal application of this "economic principle" would not only ensure the greatest returns from the least investment, it would also lead to a general economic equilibrium in which social demand matched overall supply. If one abstracts from all other social relations and views human beings solely as buyers and sellers, one may in fact construct a price system in which an equilibrium between supply and demand is achieved by virtue of the relations existing among prices. However, that is all one would have — a construct having nothing to do with reality, and no more than a rehashing, by the device of marginal analysis, of Say's discredited postulate that every supply produces its own demand. Say's theory referred to a barter economy and not to a capitalist money economy; following suit, pure price theory also relegated money to a subordinate and incidental role, since, as merely the expression of price relations, it was already taken into account in the analysis of equilibrium.

There were other money and credit theories that existed more or less on their own account, dominated by the quantity theory of money, with its assumption that price levels were dependent on the quantity of money in circulation and its velocity, that is, that they derived from the application of supply-and-demand relations to money itself. But as capital developed, its monetary system underwent corresponding developments and transformations. In the mercantile period preceding laissez-faire capitalism, both personal wealth and the wealth of nations were measured in money, and money in turn was represented by the precious metals. Although the concept of capital presumes money, it embraces all commodities just as well, with any commodity having the capacity to take the place of money. This being so, the quest for riches became contingent on the possession of capital rather than of gold or silver.

For money to function as capital, it must have ceased to be money, i.e., it must be invested in means of production and labor power from which profits in turn accrue to whomever controls production. Accumulating capital represents money values in the form of more means of production and additional labor power. Over the long run the instruments of production transfer their own value to the commodities manufactured. Of course, the mass of commodities placed on the market must be converted into money; but since they embody only a portion of existing capital, only a portion of the capital acquires money form.

In general the total sum of money needed is determined by the prices of the commodities in circulation and by the velocity of money. Of course, in order to circulate, commodities do not themselves require money but human activity and means of transportation. It is not commodities but the property claims attached to them that cause money to circulate. Any number of different forms of money may exercise this function. Commodity money, i.e., gold and silver, seems to be an expensive and unnecessary expenditure as a medium of circulation. It subserves neither production nor consumption but represents the costs of the circulation process. To produce gold and silver requires labor and capital that if put to use elsewhere would bring in profits. Of course, for the producers of gold and silver their production is as profitable as any other; but from the standpoint of society as a whole, as a means of circulation commodity money is unproductive. For this reason capital has always striven to replace commodity money with symbolic money.

Two different sorts of money came to be distinguished: commodity money and symbolic money. But historically the various money surrogates, such as bank notes and credit money, did no more than take the place of commodity money and hence remained tied to its value. Once gold-backed currencies and the international gold standard became universal, various means of payment came into use. The gold backing of paper currency was supposed to restrict its issue and hence prevent its depreciation. The gold standard also set limits on the proliferation of a nation's currency in that a country stood to lose its gold reserves if it printed too much money. In the reserve system the money in circulation was a multiple of the amount that actually had gold backing, so that at any given time only a fraction of it could be converted into gold. But as long as the confidence prevailed that the conversion was guaranteed, payment in fiat money was as effective as gold itself.

Gold is not just commodity money; because it has industrial and other uses, it is also a commodity in the simple sense of the term. Its value (and hence its price) depends on the productivity of gold production and also on the supply and demand relationships of gold. For gold and the currencies based on it to remain stable, it was necessary to control the price of gold. Originally the money value of gold and its value as a commodity were the same, but at times the commodity value exceeded the money value, and money gold was converted back into commodity gold. To keep the price of gold at a given level, that price had to be stable not only in money terms but also on the gold market. This meant that wherever the supply of gold exceeded its market demand, the excess had to be bought up by monetary authorities, whether they had need for it or not. In this way the commodity value of gold was determined by its money value.

However, the fact that the commodity value and money value of gold could be made to coincide only through state interventions or on the basis of international agreements, and further, the fact that gold as commodity money was being used less and less as a medium of circulation, gave rise to the belief that capitalists could engage in their business activities just as well without commodity money. This view had already been anticipated in Georg Friedrich Knapp's state theory of money,[2] the burden of which was that money did not need to have a value of its own, and that whatever power it had derived from the value placed on it by state fiat. However, gold-backed currency and the gold standard were maintained not merely out of tradition but because commodity money was held to be more stable. Thus commodity money circulated because it had value, and paper money had value because it circulated.

The notion of an automatic self-regulating market mechanism which at that time prevailed needed a self-regulating monetary system to go with it, and the gold standard seemed to fill the bill. The values of the various national currencies were pegged to units of account representing a specified gold content. All currencies were tied together by their gold contents, for since the price of gold was expressed per unit weight, the same quantities of gold could always be exchanged for one another. If international foreign exchange transactions did not balance out a nation's debits and credits, the outstanding payments balances between countries were cleared by gold shipments. It was presumed, or rather hoped, that these gold shipments would affect prices in the various countries in such a way that international trade relations would tend toward an equilibrium to the general benefit of all.

Under the gold standard gold flowed from countries with a negative balance of payments to countries with a positive balance. It was assumed that a gold drain from one country would lead to deflation and lower prices there, while the resultant inflation in countries acquiring gold would cause prices to rise. Sooner or later, therefore, the balance of trade of countries with low prices would improve, and that of countries with high prices would become worse, until an equilibrium in the payments balance would once again be restored. This is not the way things worked out, however. Whether the gold standard was maintained or not, capital accumulation depended on capital profitability, not on money and credit. Where expansion of money and credit boosts accumulation as a result of inflowing gold, and hence raises labor productivity, prices do not rise compared with those in countries losing gold and experiencing accumulation problems, with a consequent decline in labor productivity. The gold standard was no more an instrument of equilibrium and stability than the market mechanism, nor was it any more able to check the concentration and centralization of capital than was the domestic price system of any country.

The gold standard (like money) was not a physically necessary medium for international commodity circulation, but rather it expressed the property claims attached to commodities and capital. It seemed especially important for purposes of capital export (for loans and investments) to protect the interest and profits flowing back into a country from depreciation and losses. The capital market was concentrated in Western Europe, mainly England, and accordingly these countries were capital-exporting countries which saw to it that the gold standard retained general acceptance. It gave the different exchange rates a measure of stability and controlled national monetary and credit policies. International rivalry thus extended over money as well.

World War I spelled the end of the gold standard. Later attempts to restore it failed owing to new economic crises. With the gold standard abolished, the creation of money became the affair of each particular country. Those countries emerging defeated from the war availed themselves of inflation to cancel state debts, to divert a greater sum of surplus value into the hands of capital, to step up exploitation of the workers, and to give the capitalist economy a new boost. However, the difficulties that arose in the process eluded control, and inflation led to a total depreciation of money, sounding the imminent demise of the capitalist system. It was necessary to restore the buying power of money through the issuance of new money with no backing. The German Rentenmark, for example, had no other backing than the optimistic faith of the population in government promises to keep it stable. This was taken as patent proof that the buying power of money could be maintained even without reserves by government decree alone.

In Russia the Bolsheviks at first welcomed the inflation brought on by the war and accelerated by the revolution. For them it betokened the decay of the capitalist system. Although the issuance of paper money while the exchange rate was declining amounted to a kind of perpetual taxation, this necessity was transformed into the virtue of a monetary system that purportedly contained the seeds of its own abolition. Money, wrote Bukharin, "represents the material social weft, the fabric that holds together the whole developed commodity system of production. It is obvious that in a transitional period, as the commodity system itself is decaying, money too should lead a contradictory existence, in that, first, it undergoes depreciation, and second, the distribution of notes becomes dissociated from and independent of the distribution of products, and vice versa. Money ceases to be a universal equivalent and becomes a conventional and highly imperfect symbol of product circulation."[3]

Given the visions of a moneyless socialist economy current among the Bolsheviks at this time, the depreciation of money seemed to neatly fit their plans for reconstruction on the basis of a natural economy. But neither inflation nor barter proved to be viable solutions to the growing economic difficulties, and they were soon discarded to make way for a new monetary system. A series of currency reforms and the first steps toward a planned economy restored monetary stability, although not the relative independence money had enjoyed formerly. As a unit of payments money was transformed into an instrument of accounting and control in an economy keyed to use values and material balances. As a measure of value and a means of payment, it served the purposes of circulation only insofar as it steered commodity flows into channels specified by the plan. Its function as a medium of circulation was in general restricted to consumer income and outlays; the financial aspects of economic relations among enterprises were dealt with via the accounting procedures of the state bank.

The social regulation of production and distribution was no longer an unconscious process effected through market relationships or concretely through the circulation of money; production and distribution were henceforth controlled consciously through the medium of money, just as wage labor was used to maintain centralized control over the economy. Through the control of prices and wages, money too is controlled, inasmuch as money only expresses in figures what has already been stipulated in material terms. Money was henceforth denuded of its veil; no longer the abstract reified form of social relations, it had become a means for social control in the interests of the new modified form of capital production relations.

However, this new function of money was restricted to the domestic economy. Internationally gold continued to be required to square payments balances. According to Lenin the use of gold as building material for public conveniences was possible and appropriate only after a world socialist revolution. Until such time as that came about, it was necessary "to howl along with the wolves" and continue to produce and accumulate gold. But money gained a dual function in capitalist countries as well: an international and a domestic function; gold is considered necessary only as a universal means of payment to square outstanding payments balances.

The view has long been current that a gold-backed currency was not necessary for a nation's domestic economy. But because of traditional thinking, and out of fear of currency depreciation, commodity money was still retained. Because the gold standard set prior limits to the creation of money, these limits could just as well be defined by monetary policy. In any event commodity money lost its former importance with the development of banks and the credit system, until in the end it came to be regarded merely as an accounting unit for balancing out debits and credits. Every purchase and sale, it was now argued, created a debt that could just as well be paid through the banks without the intervention of money. Thus cashless payment transactions came increasingly to be used instead of the state-issued currency, without, however, replacing the latter entirely.

The concept of money is entailed in that of a commodity; hence gold currency was a historical although not necessary phenomenon of commodity circulation. Since all commodities are potential money and money can command any commodity, any payment medium can serve as a medium of exchange in a nation's domestic economy. For the mass of working people, money is purely a medium of exchange enabling them to exchange the commodity labor power for the commodities their wages enable them to afford. For capital, on the other hand, money is a medium of exchange as well as a medium of accumulation. A given quantity of money must be enlarged for commodity exchange to become capitalist commodity exchange. Business is not transacted to square debits and credits but to obtain profits.

The modern credit system was an instrument of rapid capital development, and capital accumulation in turn served as a powerful stimulus to the expansion of the credit system. The monetary system grew more and more complicated, although the social relations on which it was based retained their unvarnished exploitative character of capital versus labor. Today it is the banking system which is charged with implementing government money policy. Bank lending depends on the state's creation of money, which the state does by printing notes and issuing treasury bonds; it is also dependent on government-regulated reserve regulations for deposits, which, however, may vary. Though credit may be only partially covered by bank reserves, it is in general secured by the capital assets of the borrower. If there is no capital equivalent, there is also no credit. Thus it is the capital at hand, not money, which is the relevant factor.

The aim of capital accumulation is to transform a given mass of value into a larger one; accordingly, given a constant velocity, the money supply, in all its various forms, also increases. So long as capital accumulation encounters no obstacles, accumulation of value and accumulation of money take place side by side with no notable friction. But there is always a danger of a monetary crisis unfolding, since the social character of production has only one vehicle of expression, and that is the money relations of commodity production, which originate in but exist and function independently of commodity production. But aside from this ever-present possibility of a monetary crisis, a general crisis occurs only if the accumulation process is stopped or slowed; but then the crisis is always also a money crisis.

Even into the twentieth century bourgeois economics has never been able to explain crises; according to it the market mechanism should be sufficient in itself to allay any disturbances of equilibrium. But the duration and scope of the crisis between the two world wars dispelled this illusion and necessitated far-reaching economic interventions by the state. The means used were monetary and fiscal; and although they did influence the market, they did not call its existence in question. In the eyes of bourgeois businessmen and economists, the crisis was a reflection of insufficient demand, and they chose their means to combat it accordingly. Insufficient private demand had to be supplemented by public expenditures to alleviate unemployment and activate idle plant. At the same time, the profitability of private capital had to be improved so that the existing crisis and the state interventions it necessitated did not become perpetual.

Since the crisis was seen as a momentary disturbance, the measures taken to combat it were seen as something temporary as well, imposed by force of circumstances. Deficient demand caused by a reduction in new capital investments results in a lower buying power among the population or a shortage of money in general. The latter problem can be answered by inflationary means, which, however, cannot alter the accumulation difficulties that lay at the roots of the crisis. For capital inflation has a rationale only insofar as it contributes to expansion of profits on both domestic and foreign markets; it loses this rationale as the rate of inflation increases. Inflation must therefore be controlled, and this is done most effectively by deficit financing through state loans.

However, since it appeared that a growing state debt brought about by deficit financing was just as capable of expanding production as was capitalist accumulation, the notion of *functional financing* arose, the gist of which is that an economy with full employment could be regulated by state measures. This idea, which originated with John Maynard Keynes,[4] became in various versions a universal axiom. Through a combination of fiscal and monetary measures, governments, it was claimed, should be able not only to ensure full employment but also to prevent inflation and deflation. Domestically the growth of the state debt had no significance, since its assumption and payment amounted only to income transfers that would not detract from total social consumption.

This was but a variation in the altered function of money such as we see in a planned economy. Money was henceforth to function as an instrument of state economic policy within the market system. Only when the market failed in its function as an equilibrium mechanism should a nation's production be stimulated or cut back by injection or withdrawal of state-raised funds. The automatic price system would continue to be determined by consumer activity, but it would include in addition state-regulated and expanded public consumption. Since, however, increasing public consumption cuts into the amount of surplus value available for conversion into capital, a readiness to adopt this kind of economic policy required both the will and ability to disregard the accumulation needs of private capital; as, however, this would in the course of time call the capitalist system itself into question, such an economic policy can only be a temporary one, applied out of necessity and sparingly.

But a state monetary policy aimed at influencing the economy signifies at least a partial elimination of commodity and money fetishism, and in this sense it reflects the general process of decline of a market economy. It indicates an acceptance in a sense of Knapp's state theory of money and its adaptation to the mixed economic system of present vintage. But as long as the state-controlled profitless sector of the economy grows more rapidly than the private sector, the accumulation rate of the latter must fall, and such a policy of conscious, purposeful intervention into automatic market processes will not bring order into the system; its occurrence is rather a sign of decay — regardless of any temporary economic relief it may bring. Ultimately any state monetary policy meets its limits in the contradictions at work in the sphere of private production.

If it was possible to bring a nation's domestic economy out of depression by inflationary means, it was a reasonable expectation that if such means were used simultaneously in all countries no longer bound to the gold standard, the world economy as a whole would be given a boost. National monetary policies applied independently would in the process expand world trade by expanding domestic production, and international commerce could, at least in principle, be regulated just as well through international agreements without the intermediacy of gold. This idea was based on the belief, still unshaken, that under full employment the equilibrium tendencies of the market would again begin to operate at both national and international levels.

Before this could happen, however, a bitter, no-holds-barred international competition began in which every country pursued its own advantage at the expense of every other, and which finally led to World War II. The international monetary system, which had already begun disintegrating in the preceding crisis, had by this time totally collapsed and at war's end had to be rebuilt from scratch. While the war was still in progress, the victor nations met in Bretton Woods to work out the monetary foundations for the reconstruction of world trade. The Central World Bank and the International Monetary Fund were created in the light of the lessons learned from the previous monetary crises, with the aim of providing credits to prevent balance-of-payments difficulties from jeopardizing world trade.

Implicit in these measures was the old hope that the inequalities in international economic relations would in the end balance themselves out on their own, even though that might take some time. Capitalist accumulation, however, both national and international, is at the same time a process of concentration and centralization. Internationally the effects show up in the uneven development of individual capitalist countries and in shifts in their relative positions of power within the world economy. This uneven development is further accented by imperialist rivalry, giving one nation, or even one continent, the advantage of power over another. Under such circumstances one country grows rich while another grows poor, and trade relations become an instrument of international capital concentration.

The two world wars broke the hegemonic position of European capital in favor of American capital. Creditor nations became debtor nations, and vice versa. Gold shifted en masse to America, and trade relations were resumed only on the basis of long-term credits. The postwar chaos of exchange rates was replaced by a system of fixed exchange rates in parity with the gold-backed dollar, and the dollar was appointed to the status of an international money and a reserve currency. Because the dollar could be exchanged for a gold equivalent, its function as a reserve currency gave it the same status as gold. There was, however, always the danger that the price of gold would rise, which would cause all currencies to depreciate. But as long as the postwar boom continued, the likelihood of this was negligible, and the new monetary system seemed to meet the needs of the world economy as well.

Appearances were deceptive. While the vast capital destruction that had taken place in Europe and Asia made reconstruction a necessity, with a long period of economic boom ensuing, capitalist accumulation in America continued to drag its feet; anything even approximating full employment could be achieved only on the condition of government-induced supplementary production in the form of military expenditures. The result was a creeping inflation, accelerated by imperialist interventions in all parts of the world. The modest accumulation rate of American capital was a sign that the rate of profit was low; this, however, was compensated for by the exportation of capital to countries where profitability was higher. American capital export, preeminently to Western European countries, added more steam to the economic upswing already in progress and hence for some time encountered no opposition.

The monetary policies of American governments favored the export of capital and at the same time furnished the financial means for imperialist power politics. While American capitalists bought up or established whole industries in the European countries, paper dollars were being accumulated in these countries as reserves. The result was a steady flow of gold back to Europe, which meant practically that the dollar lost some of its gold guarantee. As other countries became more competitive, the U.S. positive balance of trade, which had persisted for a long time, vanished, and the negative balance that ensued could be remedied neither by trade, the return flow back into the country of profits on exported capital, nor by the export of European capital to the United States. Ultimately, if the U.S. payments deficit persisted, a breakdown of capital trade relations was inevitable.

Monetary crisis again became the catchword, and the need for a new monetary system was voiced. But these proposals were only reactions to the existing difficulties, not their solution. When the economy had failed under the gold standard, its abolition was sure, it was then said, to bring about an improvement. When floating exchange rates only deepened the chaos in world trade, fixed exchange rates were adopted again. Whereas once there was no question but that the world currency be tied to gold, now this need was disputed and free exchange rates were considered the correct policy. Monetary policy has thus invariably been but a reflex reaction to economic developments that had gone out of control. It was conscious steering of economic policy by monetary means only in the imagination of monetary theorists. If at the national level capitalist control over the economy proved to be an illusion, it turned out to be even less possible to bring international commerce under control by means of monetary arrangements. Just as state-induced full employment only conceals, but does not relieve, the crisis undermining the system, so as the capitalist system decays, it drags the monetary system along with it. And if full employment can only be achieved through inflation when accumulation is inadequate, so inflation leads through the general interdependence of the world economy to its disintegration by forcing each individual nation to try to unload its problems onto others.

Bourgeois theory tries to explain inflation with the wayward assumption that demand exceeds supply. But the number of unemployed continues to rise, more and more plant is shut down, and still inflation goes on; its cause, therefore, cannot lie simply in excessive buying power. The cause lies elsewhere: in the drive, namely, to secure capital's continued profitability despite growing public spending and the decline of instruments. The quest for more profits is also a factor determining capital exports, which are subsidized by an inflationary monetary policy. Capital must expand, and this means also geographically, with national rivalries and imperialist competition the result. Power politics is backed up by inflationary monetary policies, which are perhaps the best way to justify growing public expenditures, since they contain the promise of potential future profits. Once an inflationary course has been set and it is claimed to be the key to a specious social stability, it becomes increasingly difficult to abandon this course and return to traditional crisis mechanisms.

All warnings to the contrary, inflationary monetary policies were adopted not out of conviction but in deference to necessity. Started in the United States, they became a general phenomenon. Since a negative balance of payments in one country means a positive balance in another, the money reserves of the latter increase, and the money supply and credits expand along with them. Had the export of capital to the United States or U.S. export of its products increased commensurately, payments balances overall

could have been squared. But total American spending consistently exceeded American revenue from international economic trade. One way to meet this problem might have been to cut back on American capital exports, reduce the costs of imperialist politics, and improve competitiveness on the commodity markets at the cost of the working population; but these measures would have further undermined the already unstable American economy, which was even then dependent on inflation.

These discrepancies in capitalist economic relations are telling signs that profitability of world capital is not sufficient to enable all capitalist countries to achieve at the same time an accumulation rate permitting full employment. Each country's share in total accumulation is not constant and will fluctuate over time. Capital flows into countries with the highest profit and interest rates. Since it is the profit motive that regulates economic development, there is no way to change this process; with regard to the economic contradictions it creates, all that is left is the hope that the trend will sooner or later shift course.

If this hope is deceived, attempts are initiated to use political means to break the persistent one-sidedness of economic development; but if accumulation is insufficient, the only way this can be done is to use political force to effect a redistribution of world profits. No nation can afford over the long run to remain indifferent to the payments deficit of the world's greatest capitalist power, the ultimate consequence of which would be the collapse of world trade. All countries are as committed, if not more so, as the United States to the expansion of world trade and are therefore prepared to put aside all their reservations and make concessions that will help rescue the United States from its payments deficit. This readiness is what enabled the United States to cashier the Bretton Woods monetary system and abolish dollar convertibility.

So what had long been a national reality was now achieved on the international level as well: commodity money ceased to exist. Reserve currencies had been only partially convertible by the procedure of gold exchange based on the gold standard; but to the extent they were convertible (and that extent, moreover, was continuously diminishing), it was sufficient to prevent a general flight from currencies into gold, despite an accelerating inflation. The illusion of convertibility was sedulously maintained, e.g., through support of the official gold price (now by selling rather than buying gold), by the creation of other supposedly gold-guaranteed credits, i.e., the special drawing rights of the International Monetary Fund, and by holding the money price of gold separate from its price as a commodity. Even after dollar convertibility was abolished, the state of affairs that then arose was considered a temporary one, until such time as a new currency system could be devised in which gold would continue to play some role, if only a limited one.

The abolition of dollar convertibility and the ensuing need for a new monetary system seemed to substantiate a tendency toward a capitalist reorganization of the world economy, although with the wrong means of monetary policies, designed to bring market conditions in conformity with the needs of a more regulated world economy. In both socialist and bourgeois literature, the internationalization of capital concentration had always been linked with the abolition of money in its capitalist form. For instance, according to Hilferding, "under finance capital, capital loses its special capital character," since the ultimate outcome would be the creation of an international "general cartel." "Capitalist production will then be regulated by a central plan which determines the whole of production in all its particular spheres. Price determination will then be purely nominal, implying the distribution of the social product between the cartel-magnates on the one hand, and between the working population on the other hand. Price is then no longer a result of material relations between men, but a mere accounting devise for the distribution of goods by persons to persons. Money no longer plays a role. It can now disappear completely, for the distribution concerns itself with products and not with values. With the disappearance of the anarchic character of social production disappears the value character of commodities and therewith also money."[5] Ludwig von Mises was less captivated by, yet still was apprehensive about this development, for he too believed that a world cartel was a possibility, with the destruction of money as its consequence, since "a single world currency bank or the world cartel would be able to expand currency circulation without limit." He saw here problems which "perhaps point beyond the individualistic organization of production and distribution to new forms of collective organization of the economy of the society as a whole."[6]

At the national level it has become apparent that the market cannot be stabilized through the indirect means of monetary and fiscal policy, and that only direct measures of administrative price and income regulations could put an end to inflation. There exists then a tendency to adopt the concept of money like the one that prevails in the planned economies for the market economies as well. Although actually incompatible with the latter, since an effective price and income policy presupposes centralized control of all production and distribution, still this way of thinking indicates the undesired transformation of capitalism from an individualistic into a collective system, such as temporarily existed during times of war under the name of "war socialism."

As capitalism is disintegrating from within, so too money is becoming otiose, although the system continues to be based on it. According to Marx the accumulation and concentration of capital, and its transformation from private into share-capital would lead to a progressive socialization of capital.

> This is the abolition of the capitalist mode of production within capitalist production itself, a self-destructive contradiction, which represents on its face a mere phase of transition to a new form of production. It manifests its contradictory nature by its effects. It establishes a monopoly in certain spheres and thereby challenges the interference of the state. It reproduces a new aristocracy of finance, a new sort of parasite in the shape of promoters, speculators, and merely nominal directors; a whole system of swindling and cheating by means of corporation juggling, stock jobbing, and stock speculation. It is private production without the control of private property.[7]

In such a situation capitalist society has only its own demise ahead of it. The state is forced to intervene in the market mechanism in ways that can only paralyze it; in a word, it is constrained to apply political measures divorcing the relations of production from its market relations in order to maintain at least the former. On the other hand, as the market mechanism disintegrates, it requires on its own account government interventions to prolong its own existence, i.e., individual capital entities and corporations need the authority of the state to ensure their profitability. Economic and political measures therefore coincide; capital becomes the government, and the government spells capital. State authority, which had always been dependent on and at the service of capital, is now fully identified with capital, and its first function is to maintain the exploitative relations that market relations can no longer guarantee.

Under the hegemony of monopoly capital, the average rate of profit, which is mediated by competition, is no longer able to regulate the market mechanism. Pricing, which is done in a relatively arbitrary fashion, results in the transfer of profits from competing enterprises to the monopolies. Although this promotes capital concentration and centralization, by itself it effects no change in the total mass of profits, unless in the process the productivity of labor also increases commensurately with the needs of accumulation. If this does not occur, monopolization hinders the emergence of market relations advantageous to a progressive accumulation and gives rise to deepening contradictions on the money and commodity markets. Growing monopolization is the expression of both the rise of capital and its fall, just as accumulation heralds its beginning and its end.

Since monopolization is a product of competition, it cannot be arrested. Monopolistic pricing distributes social profits in accordance with the claims of monopolies. Thus monopolistic pricing is already the pacesetter of government distribution policy, and it is only a question of which is more appropriate: whether the state will choose the indirect way of monetary policy or the direct way of price and wage policy. However, centralized control over the entire economy, such as exists in the planned economies, cannot be achieved without the total abolition of private capital property relations. But that means a social revolution that would sweep away state monopoly capitalism. Hilferding's "general cartel" is therefore an illusion on both the national and international scale. State-capitalism destroys the economic basis for class rule for both competitive and monopoly capital, but it gives rise to a new class that rules by political means alone to assume the required control over production and distribution. Present monetary policy reflects the double-faced nature of the mixed economy, its progressive nationalization of production within existing property relations, and the resulting sharpening conflict between the real needs of society and the accumulation needs of capital. On the one hand, money is supposed to function as an instrument of deliberate and conscious economic management, but on the other it must perforce reflect existing relations of production and the resultant distribution of the social product. It is expected to serve two masters, so to speak, and in doing so serves both inadequately, as is plain from the increasingly unproductive use of labor and capital and the resultant destruction of money as the incarnation of capital production as value relations.

Domestically a nation's money is valued in terms of its buying power; it makes no difference if it is commodity money or symbolic money. Nowadays symbolic money is even coming to be regarded as superfluous, and a future is envisaged with electronic bank transactions effecting cashless and checkless payments.[8] Internationally, however, the situation is different. At least some symbolic money must be convertible into commodity money to cover the balance of payments deficits that arise in international trade. The dollar was formerly used as a reserve currency because of its convertibility into gold. But when convertibility was abolished, with it went the fixed reference point to which all currencies had been pegged; henceforth the value of these currencies depended on the shifting supply and demand situation on the market.

If the world were a single nation, the national monetary system could become an international monetary system. Commodity money and gold reserves would then be superfluous, and the money market could be controlled by government regulations. In the real world of competitive capitalist nations, however, this is not possible, and any monetary policy based on international agreements has its limits in time. Thus the fixed exchange rates of the Bretton Woods system had a stabilizing effect as long as the real instability of the world economy as a whole made every nation a debtor to the United States. But the United States was unable to maintain its position of absolute hegemony by further rapid capitalist accumulation. The reaction against the developing crisis led to a dollar inflation, with the international monetary crisis as its product.

Capitalism has been plagued by economic crises, with their accompanying monetary repercussions, throughout its history. But still the illusion persists, stronger even than before, that the conflicting interests the crisis has brought to the surface can be managed through negotiations. In the many international conferences that have been called to discuss the world monetary system, the world seems to be viewed as if it were already one nation, and words about the need for international cooperation flow on endlessly as competition grows sharper, drawing monetary policy along with it. True, the international economy has for quite a while now exhibited a degree of integration and mutual dependence such that every rising trend is felt, if to an uneven degree, throughout the world, and every serious crisis becomes a crisis worldwide as well. There is a need, therefore, for cooperation; but the way capitalism is currently organized, i.e., predominantly on a national basis, precludes hammering out any common interests that go beyond the trivial.

Thus the world monetary crisis precipitated by the abolition of dollar convertibility showed that not only generally but in monetary policy as well, national needs take precedence over international ones. The United States was neither willing nor able to abandon its inflationary course and sought to resolve its balance of payments difficulties at the expense of other nations. To a point this was quite possible, since sometimes nations are willing to endure disadvantages to avoid even greater losses. The declining competitiveness of American capital contributed to the U.S. balance of payments deficit, but this could be alleviated to some degree by the up-valuation of other currencies. Under the Bretton Woods agreements, all currencies were at parity with the dollar. Dollar inflation, manifested as a balance of payments deficit, reduced the dollar's exchange rate against other currencies. To maintain the parity of their own currencies, the central banks of other nations were obliged to buy up surplus dollars, thereby adding fuel to inflation on their own territory. To keep inflation within bounds they had to up-value their own currencies with respect to the dollar, although this made their own exports less competitive with American export products. They had to choose, therefore, between two evils: inflation, or a decline in exports. In some respects the decision was theirs, but in others it was imposed on them.

The United States was able to force the revaluation of other currencies and to make arrangements that would allow exchange rates to fluctuate over a wider range. However, the net effect of all this was only a reapportionment of world trade, with one nation's gain being another nation's loss. The volume of the world economy and profitability remained as they were. The general view now is that the present monetary crisis will be with us for some time, with temporary measures applied here and there until a new world monetary system can be fashioned that will better meet the needs of the capitalist world economy than did the former one.

It is of course an illusion to assume that a monetary system can be found that will subordinate the interests of all countries to those of the United States. The acceptance of American monetary and trade policies, whether voluntary or not, has been contingent on the relative prosperity of Japan and the Western European countries compared with the United States, and it can only be continued as long as this prosperity lasts. But signs are multiplying that a decline is already beginning that will mean these countries will no longer be either willing or able to make concessions. As long as the United States stands firm on its position that autonomous national economic policy, with its objective of more or less full employment, cannot be sacrificed to the interests and ends of a balance of payments equilibrium, other nations will be forced to maintain social stability by means of inflation and deficit financing, while at the international level resuming their competitive battle of all against all.

Of course, how this new monetary system is going to be created without squaring payments balances remains a riddle, unless the countries with positive balances are willing to toss them down the drain by writing off the deficits of other countries. In a certain sense this was in fact what already had been happening when the American deficit was translated into the monetary reserves of other countries. And although surplus dollars, in contrast to gold, flowed back onto American money markets when other nations purchased interest-bearing government bonds, that interest is not an adequate compensation for the permanent danger of further depreciations of the dollar. With no gold backing the dollar represents a claim on the United States that must diminish in value as inflation continues, whereas gold retains its value, determined as it is by production costs. Although it has been assumed that the abolition of the gold reserves would reduce the price of gold on the gold market, which has only a limited demand, it has occurred to no one to try this experiment seriously. The United States was also not willing to stand firm on dollar convertibility down to the last gold bar, but instead abolished convertibility to save what gold remained.

Even with the dollar no longer convertible, gold retains its function as commodity money. Other commodities could also perform the same function, however. More and more, suggestions are being heard that dollar surpluses should be exchanged for shares in American companies, and the Japanese central bank is considering using its surplus dollars as loans to Japanese businessmen to invest in the United States. The American deficit would thus become an instrument of capital export for other countries, as it had been in the past for America, and a balance of payments equilibrium would be effected through the proliferation of multinational concerns. If, however, nothing is changed in the existing trade relations, more deficits would bring about a further drain on American capital and make its situation, already precarious, much more so, since the profits of the multinationals would flow back into the countries of their owners. Not much is to be expected, therefore, from measures in this direction. It is more likely that attempts will be made to find compromise solutions through the International Monetary Fund, which will maintain the convertibility of the dollar into other currencies even without gold backing. The hope is still sustained that the problem will solve itself given enough time. The mechanism of artificial reserves and special drawing rights helps by gaining time; the latter was devised to utilize existing gold and currency reserves to give deficit countries a chance to square their balance of payments under long-term conditions.

But any international agreements to this end assume that current economic difficulties will not degenerate into a new world crisis. If they do, any world monetary system devised will come tumbling down, as happened in the last great crisis. World money has already gone the way of commodity money, even though the dollar must perforce continue to perform the function of a world currency without in fact being so any longer. This demise of money in its traditional form is the inevitable consequence of the dissolution of the national and international autonomy of the market and the attendant progressive decay of the capitalist economic system. These are the woes and travails of the bourgeoisie, however, although they are borne on the backs of the workers. Capital can live neither with money nor without it, and its day, like that of money itself, is long overdue. The final abolition of money will be a task for socialism to resolve.

Notes

1. *Theorie des Geldes und der Umlaufsmittel,* 1912.
2. *Staatliche Theorie des Geldes,* 1905.
3. *Ökonomik der Transformationsperiode,* 1922, p. 167.
4. *The General Theory of Employment, Interest and Money,* 1936.
5. *Das Finanzkapital,* 1910, pp. 321-22.
6. *Theorie des Geldes und der Umlaufsmittel,* p. 476.
7. K. Marx, *Capital,* Vol. 3, Kerr ed. p. 519.
8. D. W. Richardson, *Electric Money. Evolution of an Electronic Funds-Transfer System,* 1970. "There is no question," writes J. Flint in *The New York Times* of May 31, 1977, "that a revolution – or at least an evolution – is under way. The goal is to win by electronics the $1,000 billion that consumers keep in banks, savings and loan associations and credit unions, and to hold down always growing costs by eliminating paper processing. But arguments rage over the success or failure of electronic funds transfer systems – or E. F. T. as the process is known in bankers' jargon – the directions taken and the benefits or dangers for consumers. 'We have passed the point of no return,' said J. J. Poppen, a vice president of Booz, Allen & Hamilton, management consultants. 'We are reaching for the forms of full implementation, like it or not.' But he sees a final E. F. T. victory as much as a quarter century away."

1976

4

On the Concept of State-Monopoly Capitalism

In the first instance the term monopoly capitalism is no more than a correct description of existing society. Capitalism is pervaded by monopolies and in large part determined by them. The state, whose function is to protect the social structure, is thus the state of monopoly capital. This is by no means a new phenomenon in capitalist society: it has always been a feature of capitalism, if not as pronounced in the past. According to Marx, who has given us the best analysis of capitalism, capitalist competition presumes monopoly, i.e., capitalist monopoly, over the means of production. The antagonistic class relations that result from this require control of the state, which at the same time represents the national interests of capital at the level of international competition.

A capitalism of pure competition exists only in the imagination and in the models of bourgeois economics. But even bourgeois economists speak of natural monopolies and monopolistic prices. Although, granted, monopolies are not subject to the laws of the market, they are still held to be unable to shake these laws to any notable extent. Only in recent times, with whole branches of industry monopolized, has bourgeois economics been forced to deal with imperfect or monopolistic competition in its theories and to go into the changes monopoly has wrought in the market.

What for bourgeois economics marked a theoretical turn had in Marx's analysis of capital always been seen as an inherent tendency in capitalist accumulation. Capitalist competition leads to capital concentration and centralization. Monopoly was born of competition, and out of it grew monopolistic competition. Marxist theory has also always ascribed a more important role to the state than the bourgeois world was willing to acknowledge, not only as an instrument of repression but also as the organized power and mainstay of capitalist expansion.

Thus there can be nothing objectionable in the use of the term state-monopoly capitalism, although it implies no more than the simple term capitalism. Various stages can be distinguished in the process of monopolization and state economic intervention, however. Thus the development of capitalism can be represented as its progressive evolution into monopoly capitalism, and we may accordingly ask what this means in present terms, and further, what it implies for the future. It is in this context then, that emphasizing the special state-monopoly character of present-day capitalism becomes meaningful.

Capitalist accumulation tends not only toward a progressively deeper class division between labor and capital but also toward increasing concentration and centralization of the power to dispose over capital as it expands. "One capital kills many others," and what concentration is unable to achieve through competition, deliberate centralization can do through the formation of trusts, cartels, and monopolies. Capitalism thus finds itself in a state of constant change, although the underlying exploitative relations remain unaltered.

For Marx the decline of capitalism was already contained in its rise. The same social relations that allowed it to expand would also bring about its fall. Capital accumulation was a process ridden by crises; under the conditions of advanced capitalism, in which the working class is the preeminent class, every major crisis contained the possibility of social revolution. However, if we put aside revolution as a potential solution to capitalist contradictions, the trend of capitalism, despite all the setbacks during crisis periods, is toward increasing monopolization of the national economy and sharpening international monopolistic competition.

This trend is often seen as objectively preparing the way for socialism. With the transition from competition to monopoly and to the large capital units created by accumulation, concentration, and centralization, individualistic capitalist private ownership of the means of production has been transformed into the collective ownership of corporations and large concerns, in which management and ownership no longer reside in the same persons. For Marx

> capital is here directly endowed with the form of social capital (a capital of directly associated individuals), as distinguished from private capital, and its enterprises assume the form of social enterprises as distinguished from individual enterprises. It is the abolition of capital as private property within the boundaries of capitalist production itself.[1]

Whereas for Marx this situation was a sign of capitalistic decay, Friedrich Engels detected in it also a positive element, namely, a kind of capitulation of capitalistic anarchy to the planned production of the socialist future. In his view, we witness here "the reaction of the mighty, growing, productive forces against their character as capital, the increasing compulsion to recognize their social nature, which more and more forces the capitalist class itself, insofar as this is at all possible within the relations of capital, to treat them as social forces of production." Engels saw, of course, that "neither the transformation into joint-stock companies (or trusts), nor that into state-property, eliminates the capitalistic character of the productive forces. In the case of joint-stock companies (and trusts), this is obvious. And the modern state, again, is only the organization which bourgeois society provides for itself in order to support the general external conditions of the capitalist method of production against encroachments as well of the workers as of individual capitalists. The modern state, regardless of its form, is essentially a capitalistic machine, the ideal collective capitalist. The more productive forces it takes over into its possession, so much the more does it become the actual collective capitalist, and so many more citizens does it exploit. The workers remain wage-workers, proletarians. The capitalist relation is not eliminated. It is rather brought to a head. But, brought to a head it topples over. State ownership of the productive forces is not the solution of the conflict, but it conceals within it the formal means for the solution of the problem."[2]

While for Engels state property and monopolization do not eliminate capitalism's susceptibility to crises and depressions, for

Hilferding, on the other hand, their progressive development indicates the possibility of ending the capitalist crises and reducing socialism to a mere political problem. Although the pressures on all noncapitalist classes increase with increasing monopolization, nonetheless, it will finally lead to a consciously regulated social production, leaving the remaining social antagonisms to the sphere of distribution. What remained to be done would be

> the planned regulation of the economy, not by the magnates of capital and in their specific interest, but with regard to the needs of the whole society and through society. The socialized functions of financial capital — the combination of industrial and banking capital — makes the overthrow of capital so much easier. As soon as financial capital is in control of the most important branches of production, it suffices that society, by means of the proletarian state, appropriates financial capital and thereby gains control over the dominant branches of production.[3]

For Hilferding finance capital had already completed the necessary expropriation of private capital, and nationalization would merely put the finishing touches on the socialization of productive forces initiated by capital itself. Later this idea was taken up by Lenin. In his writings on imperialism he described state capitalism at the turn of the century as "parasitic, stagnating, and dying" and marked by the "substitution of capitalist monopolies for capitalist free competition. But monopoly is the transition from capitalism to a more highly developed order." Without going into Lenin's theory of imperialism, we may say that for him imperialism coincided with finance capital, and the latter was organizationally the precursor of socialism. The centralized administrative control over social capital exercised by monopoly finance had only to be taken over by the proletarian state and put to the service of society at large.

Thus we see that this concept — which goes back to Engels and was shared in common by Hilferding and Lenin despite their other differences — that monopoly capitalism paved the way for socialist society, is rooted in the false assumption that the forms of social organization accompanying capital concentration were identical with the socialization of production. Because the individual enterprise was presumed to be organized rationally and according to plan, as opposed to the irrational, unplanned functioning of the economy as a whole, Lenin imagined accordingly a socialist economy as one huge factory steered by the state. In actuality the individual firm is just as irrational as the economy as a whole, unless of course one regards the capitalist profit motive as an economically rational principle of production. Individual firms are just as dependent on the law of capital expansion as is the society as a whole and must function within the framework of general or monopolistic competition, which determines the form of their organization.

In their pursuit of profit monopolies organize themselves and no more. If they were all brought under the central control of the state, the state could do no more than reproduce this new capital relation between itself and the producers, unless of course the producers abolish the state. There is hardly any need to belabor the point further: the long existence of the "socialist states" is practical proof enough that the term socialism is no more than a cover for today's state capitalism. Complete monopoly over the means of production does not do away with the capital-labor relations; it merely frees capital from market competition without abolishing competition itself. Quite apart from the fact that competition continues to exist at the international level, even within state capitalism it merely changes its outward appearance by moving from the economic sphere into politics.

Yet so far state capitalism has been the preserve of capitalist underdeveloped countries or has been imposed imperialistically on developed countries, as in Eastern Europe; and the countries that fit Lenin's description of monopoly capitalism have remained at this stage, although the role of the state in them has grown. The conditions of a monopolistically controlled world market precluded any possibility of capitalist development by way of competition for the underdeveloped countries. In a situation more or less similar to the prerevolutionary status in Russia, that is, with a weak bourgeoisie, a proletarian minority, and a predominantly agrarian population, these nations could only counter the head start of the monopolistic nations by establishing even more rigid monopolistic control over economic life. Monopoly capitalism evokes state capitalism not within monopolistic economies but in the struggle against them.

Indeed, Russia's example has shown that a state-controlled economy is able to speed up industrialization, at least in large nations, even if only at the expense of the working population and to the benefit of state capitalism's newly spawned ruling class.

Prompted by the major role played by the state in the war economies of World War I, Lenin was led to regard monopoly capitalism, with its imperialist imperative, as state monopoly capitalism, in which the state serves the monopolies. The next step in the direction of socialism in capitalist countries would then accordingly be to sever the state's ties to monopoly interests and reorganize it to serve the interests of the population as a whole. First, however, it was necessary to smash the state of the monopolists to make way for a new state, which could then get down seriously to the task of abolishing capitalist exploitation. State-monopoly capitalism was to give way to the socialist state, without losing thereby its centralized administrative control over the economy at large. Leninists still adhere to this program, although it amounts to nothing more than the attempt to drive out the devil with Beelzebub.

With state capitalism identified with socialism, regarded as a transition to a stateless communism set sometime in the far-distant future, the struggle for socialism becomes a struggle against present-day state-monopoly capitalism. This struggle can only be a revolutionary struggle, since state-monopoly capitalism will hardly hand in its resignation voluntarily. Although state capitalism still continues worker exploitation, it nevertheless does destroy the class domination of the bourgeoisie. But the communist parties in the Western nations, which now appear to have taken up the banner against state-monopoly capitalism, had ceased as long ago as 1920 to be a revolutionary movement. They are no longer prepared to put through their own program by revolutionary means, and they are waging a mock battle against state-monopoly capitalism in order to gain for themselves places of influence within the existing systems.

This is not to say that the Western communist parties have abandoned their own goals. Whenever and wherever the opportunity presents itself, one can be sure they will attempt to divert every successful anticapitalist movement in the direction of state capitalism. Since such movements are not yet on the agenda, these parties pour all their efforts into a struggle for positions of power within the existing society, and their "struggle" against state-monopoly capitalism becomes an empty propagandistic slogan to mobilize the masses behind them, masses as yet turned only against the "bad sides of capitalism," not against capitalism itself. Indeed, the communist parties are neither against capitalism nor against the state; they are only against a state that is wholly in the services of the monopolies and for a state and a capitalism that serve the common interest.

But a common interest can only exist under classless socialism. Under capitalism there exist only irreconcilable class interests. Therefore capitalistically inclined social strata that are the victims of monopolization cannot be won over to socialism because their special social positions would be destroyed even more rapidly and thoroughly under it than under monopoly capitalism. At most they can be won over to a capitalist program that caters to their special interests, in a word, an antisocialist policy. Thus behind the slogan of a struggle against state-monopoly capitalism lurks the proclamation of a counterrevolutionary policy directed against socialism.

It is, however, quite conceivable that as monopolistic pressure intensifies, driving segments of the petite bourgeoisie into the proletariat, some of these petit bourgeois layers will be persuaded that their last chance lies with state capitalism, which they hope will throw open the gates to the career monopoly capitalism had barred to them; one glimpse into the "socialist countries" is sufficient to confirm their optimistic expectations. However, for the workers the same glimpse gives a somewhat different picture. They have no burning desire for this kind of socialism. Therefore for them communist policy, in countries where it carries some weight, e.g., in France or Italy, does not represent the embodiment of the desire for the revolutionary transformation of state-monopoly capitalism into state capitalism, but their only immediate interests

within the existing social system. The functions of the communist parties are reformist, not revolutionary, and ultimately, therefore, they serve to sustain the continued existence of state-monopoly capitalism.

In the light of this situation, the sham struggle against state-monopoly capitalism is only a slogan of embarrassment. The communist parties have for a long time now been unwilling to mount an offensive against capitalism itself on either a national or an international scale — "peaceful competition" and the business ties between the different social systems are proof enough of this. At the national level they take pains to assure that they are against only the self-seeking uncurbed power of the monopolies, not against the state or capitalism itself, and that state involvement is required to bring the monopolies under state control. At the international level the alleged struggle against state-monopoly capitalism serves the ends of an opportunistic imperialist policy. They are not against imperialism as such, only against the imperialist policies of other nations, which serve the interests of their national monopolies to the disadvantage of their own country's imperialist or national interests. The distinction between capitalism and state-monopoly capitalism can be used to justify either alliances or hostilities between the "socialist" and the capitalist countries, as well as differences among the "socialist" countries themselves. In other words, the communist parties utilize the slogan of struggling against state-monopoly capitalism only to conceal their own capitalist, hence imperialist, policy and to win the support of the workers.

The "theory" of state-monopoly capitalism serves, then, on the one hand, as an apology for the totally reformist activity of the communist parties in the capitalist countries and, on the other hand, the changing demands of imperialist power politics; it gives notice, therefore, that despite all their points of difference, both capitalist and "socialist" countries have taken upon themselves the joint task of defending capitalist production relations against any socialist transformation. This is nowhere more obvious than in the current convergence theory, ostensibly rooted in industrialization, which seeks to obliterate the differences between these two different social systems. Since the industrialization process is the same under both state capitalism and monopoly capitalism, the social formations, according to this theory, differ only in the degree of centralization of administrative control over social production and distribution. But since under state-monopoly capitalism this administrative control has already brought about a separation between ownership and management, only a small step remains to complete the transformation of private capitalism to state capitalism, one that can be accomplished politically. With this step achieved, socialism will have been born out of capitalism, marking the end of social class struggles.

Furthermore, since nothing else need be changed in the existing system of production aside from abolishing the monopolies, there is nothing in the system that should not be adequate to the needs of socialism as well. This explains the relative indifference shown today toward the recurrent crises of present-day capitalism. The blame for the difficulties and injustices with which it continues to be beset is laid on the state, which has assumed the interests of the monopolies as its own interests. Therefore merely another state or another government, not a different economic system, is what is required. Present-day capitalism and state capitalism experience a meeting of the minds on this point as well. State-monopoly capitalism also imagines that it, too, has put an end to crises through state interventionist policies. As this illusion steadily loses credibility in the face of the hard facts, opposition to state-monopoly capitalism adopts the goal of a broader, and in the end a total, state control of the economy to avoid further convulsions.

As among the bourgeoisie itself, a capitalist solution is sought to capitalist contradictions. The "left" is prepared to sacrifice monopolies to save capitalism. The bourgeoisie has long ago given up belief in automatic regulation of the economy through the market. As competition peters out, prices and profits are no longer determined by the market but set at will by the monopolies. Since, however, nothing can be changed in the monopolistic structure of the economy, the state must intervene not only to ensure full employment through money and fiscal policies, but also to regulate wages and prices in the interests of economic stability. It is the task of the state to achieve by political means what the capitalist market is unable any longer to achieve by itself. Indeed, state intervention h~~ grown steadily, and state economic policies were given credit for periods of economic prosperity, prompting the notion that capitalism actually was susceptible to rational control.

Socialist theories had anticipated this view. Hilferding wrote, for instance:

> The monopolistic elimination of competition also eliminates the objectively given price relations. Prices cease being objective magnitudes and become a mere instrument of account for those who consciously determine what the prices should be. The realization of the Marxian doctrine of capital concentration in monopoly capitalism eliminates also the Marxian labor theory of value.[4]

What Hilferding did not see was that in Marx's theory of value, the law of value determined only the general price level and its fluctuations, not prices themselves. Competition *tends* toward an average rate of profit, which is the resultant of deviations between price and value. Surplus profits or monopoly prices have been a constant feature throughout all of capitalist development and one of the reasons for accelerated accumulation. As monopolization progresses, monopoly prices reduce the average rate of profit of competing capitals. Profits here are transferred from the sphere of competition to the sphere of monopolies. As competition declines, the possibility of transferring profits from the competitive sector to the monopoly sector of the economy also diminishes; through the law of value the monopolistic rate of profit tends to become the average rate of profit.

A monopolistic economy does not abolish the law of value; on the contrary, it reaffirms it, since the rate of profit and hence the rate of accumulation continue to fall under monopoly capital as well, necessitating state intervention in the economy. But such interventions are limited by capitalist production relations themselves and can only be seen as short-term measures. Once their possibilities are exhausted, the capitalist crisis cycle resumes, and once again the revolutionary transformation of the capitalist system becomes a real possibility. Under state-monopoly capitalism, as under capitalism in any other form, the task of the proletariat remains one and the same, namely, the abolition of capitalist relations through the elimination of wage labor in a classless society.

Notes

1. K. Marx, *Capital,* vol. 3, Kerr ed., p. 516.
2. F. Engels, *Anti-Dühring*, Kerr ed., pp. 288-90.
3. R. Hilferding, *Finance Capital,* p. 502.
4. Ibid., p. 313.

1973

5

State Capitalism and the Mixed Economy

Marx's *Capital* bears the subtitle *Critique of Political Economy* to show that it was intended as a critique of capitalist society and of the economic theories arising out of it. The critique is made from the standpoint of the working class, that is, from its place in the production process, on which the capitalist mode of production and its laws of movement rest. When workers won the ten-hour day, Marx hailed this as a victory of the "political economy of the workers," implying that the opposition between capital and labor determined not only the real economic processes but political economy as well. As long as the class struggle is fought on the terrain of political economy, it remains within the capitalist relations of production. To be done with these relations, the capital-labor relation, and hence political economy, must be abolished as well.

Up to now the class struggle has been fought on the terms of political economy. To pass beyond this limitation requires a revolutionary transformation and a classless society. As long as this limitation exists, a *practical* critique of political economy can be but partly successful, since the reproduction of capital involves the reproduction of the class and production relations inherent in it. For its continued existence capital presupposes accumulation, which the class struggle may influence but cannot abolish. Non-accumulating capital signals a state of crisis, which will either lead to a revolutionary situation or set the stage for a new phase of accumulation by altering the capital-labor relation, i.e., the relationship between value and surplus value. The drive to accumulate does not preclude periods of stagnation; these must be overcome, however, if capital is not to suffer its demise in social struggles. Until that happens the class struggle of political economy is not only the terrain on which one class gains victory over or meets defeat at the hands of the other, it is also a driving force of capitalist development. The reduction of labor time also implied the transition from absolute to relative surplus value production. The related increase in labor productivity increased surplus value despite reduced labor time, with the result that the proletariat was gradually able to improve its living standards as capitalism continued to accumulate. Since, however, there are also limits to the production of relative surplus value, accumulation remains subject to the capitalist crisis cycle.

In periods of rapid capital expansion, the social contest is restricted to the struggle for higher wages, better working conditions, and a social policy agreeable to the workers. In a bourgeois democracy the economic struggle also assumes political garb to oblige the state to comply with the limited interests of the workers. The work of trade unions in the economic sphere is complemented in the political sphere by the activity of political labor organizations that seek to influence the state. Although the reproduction of capitalist production relations may preclude any fundamental change in society, the state nonetheless still has the means, or so it seems, to intervene in economic matters. The conquest of state power, therefore, commended itself as an appropriate means for transforming society.

For Marx the state was an instrument of class rule, which included state functions that, although they did not directly pertain to securing the existing social structure, were nonetheless dictated by the asocial character of capitalist production. It was part of the functions and tasks of the state to maintain the general conditions of production, which do not necessarily ensue from the competition among private capital entities, and to safeguard the interests of national capital in international competition. The diversity of state functions gives the appearance that the condition of the state is one of relative independence from capital. Individual capital entities are still subject to the jurisdiction of the state, whose task as an instrument of capital in general is to secure the accumulation conditions of nationally organized capital entities and hence to maintain the exploitative relationship between capital and labor. Since, however, there is no such thing as capital "in general" — it being no more than the totality of individual capitals — capitalist society needs the state to protect the interests of the ruling class.

The relationship between state and capital is based on capitalist relations of production, i.e., exploitation. The state survives on surplus value, whether directly or indirectly appropriated. The interests of the state, even in its condition of relative independence, are identical with the interests of capital. The state assumes exploitation and hence class relations. In the Marxian sense, therefore, socialism implies not a socialist state but in fact the abolition of the state as a social institution.

Since the state has a share in the total social surplus value, surplus value is distributed not only by way of capitalist competition but also by political means. Placing checks on state appropriation of surplus value has always been one of the aims of bourgeois politics. Cheap governments mean better chances for accumulation. Still, as capital accumulated the state's share in social surplus value also increased: the means of control over the potential domestic enemy had to be expanded, while imperialist competition absorbed ever growing amounts of surplus value. But since capital accumulation also means concentration and centralization, and competitive capitalism is thereby transformed into monopoly capitalism, as a result, it becomes more and more difficult to establish an average rate of profit and hence to effect the allocation of output by means of the market alone, although it is this market allocation that serves as the lifeline ensuring the harmony of individual capital entities with total capital. More and more the task of allocating surplus value became the object of state interventions in the economy.

It was this situation which at the turn of the century produced a veritable epidemic of notions about a state-monopoly economy for which boundless possibilities were proclaimed or which, on the other hand, was declared to contain the seeds of its own destruction. For Rudolf Hilferding, for instance, the capitalist concentration process was tending ultimately toward a "general cartel" in which industrial capital and bank capital would be fused, laying the necessary foundations for central economic planning. The abolition of competition by finance capital would bring about permanent economic equilibrium, and capitalist crises would be no more. State control, i.e., the shouldering of the economy by the state, would then complete the transformation of capitalism into socialism. Since, however, the bourgeois state is the instrument of capital and abolition of competition at the national level is accompanied by stepped-up competition internationally, from Hilferding's theory, which was otherwise generally accepted, Lenin drew different conclusions. For him modern capitalism signaled the marriage of the state with finance capital, and that was the situation which had to be overcome in order to accelerate the advent of the social revolution fermenting in the process of disintegration imperialism had engendered; a new state, its roots planted firmly in the dictatorship of the proletariat, would then proceed to make a socialist economy a reality.

Although their points of emphasis differed, for Lenin as for Hilferding the state was the vehicle whereby the transition from capitalism to socialism would be effected. The terms "state capitalism" or "state socialism" each referred to a situation existing within capitalist society and preceding a socialist revolution. Elements of state capitalism, so went the argument, evolved in contradiction with bourgeois society, and were hence to be viewed as symptoms of disintegration. They signaled the abolition of private capital within a private capitalist economy and reflected both the dynamic movement of the productive forces relative to static property relations and the growing need for deliberate, conscious socialization of production. But to achieve this — to transform capitalism shot through with state-capitalist elements into socialist society — private ownership of the means of production, and hence wage labor, would have to be abolished.

One must keep in mind the original distinction between state capitalism and socialism, that is, between the tendency, unfolding within capitalist society, toward an increasing state production of surplus value and state interventions in the market, on the one hand, and on the other, socialist revolution, which would abolish the capital-labor relationship and effect the transition from a market economy to an economy based on social needs. Even in the evolutionary conception of reformism, state capitalism was supposed to transform itself by means of its own quantitative expansion into the qualitatively new state of socialism. For revolutionary socialism state capitalism was only a modification of capitalist production relations that altered nothing in its antisocialist character; capital had to be abolished in all its forms.

Initially these were only speculations about the future, since neither state capitalism, as a dominant form of society, nor socialism existed. They gained a measure of timeliness first with the Russian Revolution, which found itself confronted with the problem of building socialism. Lenin observed rightly enough that the socialist movement had not dealt seriously with the question of the actual building of socialism, nor indeed could it have done so, since it was impossible to foresee under what specific conditions the social revolution would be achieved. One had, therefore, to start out from the situation as it was given, which in the case of Russia, of course, meant a situation of underdeveloped capitalism. Consequently there could be no thought initially of socialization of the means of production or of the conditions of production, in any event not for the peasantry, who were crucial to the revolution; for the time being one could only make use of state power to accelerate the pace of industrialization, as it alone was the means by which the material conditions for socialism would be created.

However, Lenin did not view the Russian Revolution as an isolated phenomenon; for him it was but one aspect of a worldwide revolutionary process. Uneven development among nations was a feature of capitalism, which, of course, detracted in no way from capital's world dominion. Likewise, the uneven development of socialist countries would not, according to Lenin, impede the establishment of socialism on an international scale; in fact, it should even help matters, since the great mass of the world's population could secure their own interests only by struggling against imperialistic capitalism. International solidarity was the key to overcoming the backwardness of the underdeveloped countries in order then to proceed to the construction of a worldwide socialist economy.

Expectations of world revolution aside, the conditions in Russia, inauspicious as they were, remained the Bolsheviks' point of departure in their formulation of economic policy. With the exception of nationalizing the banks and foreign trade, the Bolsheviks initially did not intend to expropriate capital; they wanted to place it under state control. Lenin's model was centralized state control over production and distribution, as exemplified by the German war economy during World War I.

But neither capitalists nor workers were pleased with this strategy of reconstructing a state-steered economy. The period of "workers' control" and capitalist sabotage met an early end and forced the state to expropriate the factories.

We need not go here into all the zigs and zags of Bolshevik economic policy; they are sufficiently well known. We should be clear, however, that this policy was imposed on the Bolsheviks by force of circumstances, and it was only afterward that a theoretical apology was produced for it. "Heroic war communism," as long as it lasted, was thus proclaimed the true way to communism; but it was then downgraded to the status of a temporary expediency after it collapsed. The next stage, the New Economic Policy, which partially restored the market, was regarded, at least by Lenin, as a step backward from a consistent policy of socialization, although at the same time it was considered an unavoidable transitional phase from capitalism to communism. Soon, however, it appeared to be obstructing this transition and even to be calling into question Bolshevik state power as a necessary prerequisite for it. The solution to the problem lay, it was hoped, in the sacking of the New Economic Policy and the forced collectivization of agriculture, which was then to be placed under state control. Only then did it become unmistakably clear where the theory and practice of Bolshevism could lead.

The consolidation of the new social economic relations, which have taken their place in history under the name of Stalinism, was regarded as a stage along the way from capitalism to communism and was called socialism. Socialism was a transitional society, it was argued, and as such would still be plagued by many of the features of capitalism; however, it anticipated many of the characteristics of communism as well. In the list of capitalist features that had not yet been overcome were the existence of the state, the social division of labor, and unequal distribution, justified on the basis of the nonequivalence of work performed. What distinguished socialism from capitalism was, first, the abolition of private ownership of the means of production and, second, economic planning. Full communism presupposed world revolution, but a real possibility existed for the building of socialism, at least in each country. Not to be identified with either capitalism or communism, socialism was a new social order that could lead to communism, since socialization of the means of production and conscious control of production and distribution made a reversion to private capitalism impossible. While in Marxist theory it was the producers themselves who controlled the means of production in order to put them to use socially, in Bolshevik theory it was the state, as guardian of the interests of the producers, which held the reins of power over the means of production and thus over production and distribution. The theory of the political party as representative of workers' interests in the social revolution was now being applied to socialism. The means of production kept the attributes of property but had now become state property, and presumably later would become social property. The step from private property to state property was supposed to represent the transition from capitalism to socialism.

A new type of society had undoubtedly come into being. Although not communist according to traditional socialist conceptions, it was also not capitalist in the traditional sense. Socialism had always implied the end of private capital, and state control over the means of production laid the groundwork for that. Production relations are social relations, and in the historically unfolding relationship between capital and labor, it had been workers against capitalists. Accordingly the abolition of this relationship looked like the end of capitalist relations of production as well; from the standpoint of the capitalists who had been expropriated by the state, there was no doubt, at any rate, that the new social order was identical with the end of capitalism, whatever name, socialism or communism, might be given to it.

From the workers' standpoint, however, essentially nothing has changed. The means of production, now state property, still elude their grasp. The producers are still wage laborers and still have no influence over production and distribution. The how and what of production are still decisions beyond their control, to be made by state institutions, the self-proclaimed caretakers of the interests of society. But society remains divided into a group of persons organized under the state who control the conditions of production and the mass of the population, which must follow their directives. Thus the relations of production remain class relations, in which those holding privileged positions by virtue of their control over the state have assumed the functions of the expropriated bourgeoisie.

For the expropriated bourgeoisie this new type of society, characterized by state control over the means of production, is state socialism or socialism pure and simple; for the workers, however, the capital relationship still persists and is fittingly described by the term "state capitalism," although ideologically it tries to pass itself off as socialism. The expropriation of private capital distinguishes state capitalism from the state-capitalist features already discernible within capitalism. State capitalism, disguised as socialism, presupposes a revolutionary transformation from private capitalism. The state-capitalist tendencies that begin to emerge within traditional capitalism do not evolve gradually into state capitalism; a revolutionary abolition of private capital is required.

The *de facto* abolition of private capital gives rise to the erroneous assumption that socialization and state appropriation of the means of production are one and the same thing. But according to socialist theory, the state is an instrument of class rule, and therefore in a classless socialist society it should become superfluous. Those central authorities still necessary would perform only technical and organizational, not state, functions and would remain dependent on the decisions of the producers. This conception does not fit the state-capitalist system. Under "socialism" it is the state alone which makes political and economic decisions to fend off the internal and external perils yet remaining along the path toward communism. The state in the traditional sense would disappear only in the far distant future, after the world revolution had been accomplished and a communist economy established throughout the world.

In "socialist" practice it is the state and the state institutions created by and subordinate to it which control production and distribution. The state is shaped by the political party in possession of state power, that is, by a privileged stratum of society that believes itself capable of representing the interests of society as a whole and able to do what is needed to realize those interests. Its existence and its power of decision over society and its development presuppose control over how total output will be allocated among the producers, state institutions, and the requirements of expansion, i.e., the needs of social reproduction. The wage system, taxation, and the administrative manipulation of prices place a surplus product in the hands of the state; or in other terms, the producers are deprived of control over their surplus labor, which the state appropriates. Surplus labor, which under capitalism appears as surplus value, is thus appropriated directly, not by the exchange of goods, although the wage nature of labor sustains the illusion that exchange relations still exist. Since, however, the "political economy of the workers" is abrogated under authoritarian "socialism," it is the state that continues to determine surplus labor.

Marx himself pointed out that surplus labor is unavoidable, since the needs of society extend beyond the needs of the direct producers. It is not the existence of a surplus product, therefore, which distinguishes capitalism from socialism but how that product is appropriated socially, and that is a question decided by control over production. Under capitalism surplus labor appears as surplus value; its distribution is regulated by competition and modified by monopolization. Since capitalist production is controlled by accumulation, and the latter must take place under competitive conditions, capital is unable to exercise control over surplus value. Accumulation does not depend on capitalists but on the mass of surplus value, which to them is an unknown quantity, in relation to social capital. The rate of profit determines the possibility or impossibility of capitalist accumulation. It is therefore not only exploitation or the production of surplus value which weighs on the workers but also capital's inherent need to expand; however, from time to time this need cannot be met, and the very existence of the workers, the producers of surplus value, is placed in jeopardy. The crisis nature of capitalist production is patent proof that capitalism cannot even satisfy its own "social" needs, to say nothing of genuine human needs.

State-capitalist systems have, at least in theory, the means to regulate consciously what share of social production must go to the workers and the amount of surplus labor to be placed at the disposal of the state. As in capitalist society, the size of the surplus labor depends on the share of total output passed on to the producers. In contrast to capitalism, however, the use of surplus labor is no longer determined by competition and the need to accumulate but becomes the conscious decision of the state. Reproduction can therefore take place independently of capital's inherent need to expand, i.e., it no longer depends on a specific mass of surplus value or a specific rate of profit but may be accomplished with any given amount of surplus product; or, if the surplus product is not sufficient, reproduction may be maintained at a steady level without that necessarily causing a crisis.

On this feasible conjecture rests the belief that a socialist state, which represents the general interests, can shape production and reproduction in such a way that surplus labor becomes a part of necessary labor and is no longer the product of exploitation. The state does only what the producers themselves would do if they acted on their own. They too would have to create the institutions and facilities proffered them by the state; it follows "logically," therefore, that the interests of the state coincide with the interests of the producers.

In a "state-capitalist model," moreover, in which the state is the sole executive organ for society's needs, its functions would no longer be state functions; the system would then cease being state capitalist. In the present state-capitalist countries, the state, however, determines social relations; it sets itself apart from society in order to impose its will on it. It is obvious that the will of the state should be identified with the needs of society, if only because the state is dependent on it. This dependence forces it to act as a state in the traditional manner, i.e., to employ coercive means to maintain and secure its own material conditions of existence.

The state consists of persons who hold the reins of power, and hence control production and distribution. Once this situation exists, social reproduction means reproduction of state power as well; and the growth of social wealth means, of course, the expansion of the power of the state. As time goes on it becomes inconceivable that reproduction could take place other than in the existing social relations, for this would require a fundamental reorganization of the society. The division of society into a minority that determines everything and a majority with no influence signifies a class relation which the privileged strata defend just as obdurately as they have done in other class societies.

This situation has nothing to do with an "immutable human nature," which may permit one elite to take the place of another but would never allow the abolition of class relations; the plain fact is that even in the purportedly "socialist" revolutions of the past, the task of reorganizing society was left to the state, the party, and hence an elite. The rebelling population acquired their political experience within organizational forms that had been shaped by the class nature and political economy of capitalist society and hence could not measure up to the requirements of a classless society. Revolutionary means were used to reformist ends, namely, the restoration of a collapsed economic system with the aid of new political institutions. Abolition of the existing production relations was not contemplated; rather attention was concentrated on effecting needed changes within the framework of the existing production relations, which the former ruling class had been unable to manage because of its particular class interests. These social movements were therefore not proletarian revolutions that had their sights set on the abolition of class relations; but neither were they demonstration nor proof of the impossibility of such revolutions.

A revolution is genuinely a proletarian revolution if it objectively rules out the possibility of both the continuation of the old and the emergence of new class relations. Traditions are obstacles to deep-going changes; but the recent experiences with state-capitalist systems indicate that the dictum that the "liberation of the working class" can only be "the work of the workers themselves" is more than a mere phrase; it spells out the primary prerequisite of socialist society. The workers must create their own organizational forms out of the capitalist production relations and overthrow the latter to establish a classless society. The organization and control of production and distribution must remain in the hands of the producers; the establishment of a new state with an autonomous power position must be prevented. The experiments of the council communists showed, if only in vague form, the direction the proletariat's struggle for emancipation must take, although they still lacked the concrete basis on which to bring this about. But whatever the difficulties facing socialism, the existing state-capitalist systems have proven that their way, in any event, is not the way to socialism.

But is state capitalism a necessary stage of development after capitalism — can it not be avoided? State capitalism did, after all, arise in underdeveloped capitalist countries — apart from those countries which fell under the Russians' sphere of influence as the spoils of war and were trimmed and tailored to conform to the Russian model of state capitalism, with varying degrees of success. All the same, notwithstanding the fact that state capitalism was imposed on these countries from without, they do demonstrate that state-capitalist production relations can be implanted in developed and underdeveloped countries alike. Also, the growing trend toward state intervention in the capitalist countries seems to be pointing the way toward a transition to state capitalism, if not by way of revolution then at least through a perceptible convergence of the two systems.

The uneven development among nations, stressed by Lenin, within the imperialist-dominated world economy has created links between the anti-imperialist national revolutionary movements and the anticapitalist movements in imperialist countries. It has also served to underscore the difficulties, if not the impossibility, of independent capitalist development in the colonies and in other underdeveloped countries. The industrial nations' head start in accumulation and their monopolistic positions within the world economy seem to preclude capitalist development by the competitive route in the backward and suppressed countries. Subordinated to the profit claims of the major capitalist powers, the way toward independent industrialization and capital accumulation was essentially barred to them. Capitalist development, and its handmaiden industrialization, could be achieved only via the political route of nationalist revolutions; that is, not through the bleak and arduous process of formation of capitalist private property, but as the outcome of the confrontation between monopoly capital and capitalist monopoly.

The Russian Revolution took place in a backward capitalist country with a weak bourgeoisie; indeed, Lenin regarded this as the reason why it was relatively easy to achieve. Being directed against capitalist imperialism, national revolutionary movements were committed to an anticapitalist ideology and, under the influence of Russian Bolshevism, equated their state-capitalist aspirations with "Marxist socialism." Russian Bolshevism was the product of the European labor movement and as such saw itself as a world, not a national, revolutionary movement. But the revolution remained within national confines and, cramped as it was, became the model other national revolutionary movements followed. The important point here is that this emulation of the Russian experience has been the identifying characteristic of all viable national revolutionary movements since. State control over national production and distribution, the idea the Bolsheviks took from the capitalist war economy, has in any event been the programmatic goal of state-capitalist-oriented countries.

State intervention, a policy forced on capitalism by the war, was used by the Bolsheviks to build up their own economic system, but its subsequent fate has had political and economic repercussions on the further course of capitalist development. The totalitarian state that flowed from the dictatorship of the party became the prototype of the fascist and national socialist movements that put in their appearance in the aftermath of World War I. A totalitarian state may just as well defend an economic system based on private enterprise. Fascism and National Socialism adapted Bolshevik methods and the Bolshevik party-state to defend their own interests as well as those of private capitalist society. In the defeated and economically weaker countries, it looked as if the postwar crisis had called into question the very existence of capital. Since, however, the Russian Revolution did not spread across Europe, the crisis situation required national solutions within the framework of the capitalist world economy. The national solution, like the war economy before it, could not be left to the automatic workings of the market but required major interventions in the economy, which of course meant expanding and strengthening the powers of the state.

When the postwar crisis developed into a general crisis of capitalism rather than into a new worldwide boom, the bourgeois liberal or "democratic" countries were themselves forced to employ extreme state measures to cope with the social hazards created by the crisis. The fascist countries pursued the path of Bolshevism, and the "democratic" nations followed suit to help embattled capitalist production relations through the crisis. However, in the democratic states there was no need to put an end to the "political economy of the workers," inasmuch as they were able to employ other means to put through the economic policies they thought necessary. The fascist tendencies in these countries were thus undercut and could not exploit the crisis for their own ends. State interventionism thus ranged over a wide field: from the direct takeover of the means of production by the Bolsheviks, to fascist use of the state to sustain capitalist production relations, and finally to state steering of the business cycle by the indirect means of monetary and fiscal policies.

The "purely economic" anticyclic measures of the democratic countries were, of course, also part and parcel of fascist economic policy; but in the party dictatorships of the totalitarian states, they were complemented by political action in the domestic sphere as well as in foreign policy. Dictatorship as a means to carry on capitalist production relations is obliged to subserve the expansionist needs of state capital, with new imperialist conflicts the inevitable result. It was the repercussions of fascism on foreign policy that troubled the victors of World War I, not its domestic policies, which enjoyed their silent approval. Although capitalist economists now saw that the market mechanism was not capable of coping with the crisis, there was no question of their sitting back passively as they watched social unrest grow after the war, since the Bolshevik experiment and fascism were practical proof enough that under very different conditions (and not only under socialism, i.e., state capitalism), the effects of crisis, e.g., unemployment and idle means of production, could be combated if the state were willing to take the appropriate measures.

According to the market theory, which though false is nonetheless needed by capital, crisis was rooted in a lack of effective demand, which in turn had its origins in capitalist growth itself. In this view, of course, consumption determines production, from which it follows that an increasing saturation of consumer needs must result in a slackening of production and hence a decline in investments. The consequence is unemployment and idle capital. In bourgeois theory the market and prices function as equilibrium mechanisms, in which each production factor is guaranteed its share of total production; accordingly the dilemma of crisis cannot be resolved through redistribution lest this be at the cost of capital returns, which were already on the decline, further undercutting the propensity to invest. The market, therefore, cannot be expected to generate the demand required for full employment; that demand, rather, must be created from without, through state-induced public demand, and added to general demand.

State-induced public demand could not, however, be financed by taxation, since this would have reduced market demand, already insufficient, even more. Thus, as in wartime, deficit financing, the expansion of state credit, was the answer. By means of government loans and their use for public works, idle capital was brought back into the capitalist circulation process to boost total production. The result of this, of course, was a growing state debt, which, however, was not considered a burning problem as long as total production grew at a faster rate than the interest burden on it.

In contradiction to bourgeois consumption theory, which projects the inevitable collapse of the market system, state economic intervention by way of induced public demand was seen as an anticyclic policy that would maintain — or restore — market equilibrium. Yet it is patent that capital accumulation precludes equilibrium between supply and demand in terms of an equivalence of production and consumption. In a capitalist economy good times with full employment are possible only as a result of capital expansion in pursuit of profits. When there is no accumulation, insufficient demand is a permanent condition. It is not enough, therefore, merely to expand production and to adjust demand to supply. For accumulation to take place, the profitability of capital must be improved. Its own static theory notwithstanding, in the real economic process bourgeois economics is also obliged to propose state-induced demand to generate an additional demand in order to expand the market.

State economic policy was supposed to prevent the major economic ups and downs, i.e., crises as well as booms, which undermine the economic equilibrium.

In addition to the manipulatory measures of expanding or contracting public demand, monetary policy, i.e., the expansion or contraction of credit by means of increasing or reducing the money supply and by altering interests rates, was supposed to have a regulatory effect on the economy. The instruments of state intervention in a modified market economy are too well known to require further discussion here, but together they spell what has come to be known as a "mixed economy," vaunted as the solution to the problem of capitalist crises.

The idle capital made available to the state by means of loans represents an already existing surplus value that had not been put to use as further profit-generating capital. It puts idle people and plant to work; the resulting product is not sold on the market but matches the value of the state's loans. In this way money capital is "consumed" and hence can no longer be regarded as a part of the mass of surplus value available to capital for purposes of accumulation. Here capitalist society produces not in accordance with its own needs but in accordance with its own false theory, i.e., it produces for consumption, if only public consumption. In that event, however, this type of production is no longer capitalist production but the employment of an anticapitalist mode of production — possible only in exceptional cases, never as the rule.

The expansion of state credit, like any other form of credit expansion, carries with it an inflationary trend which, however, can to some extent be controlled at the price of limiting state-induced production, a general contraction of credit, and the cooling-off effect this has on economic activity. A "mixed economy," therefore, tends toward its own dissolution, and capital is once again placed at the mercy of its own crisis cycle. The theory that boasted of having mastered the problem of crisis itself has a new crisis on its hands in which the instruments of a mixed economy are not only of no use but indeed even help to deepen the crisis. Instead of achieving full employment, even with its inflationary tendency, by monetary and fiscal policies and public spending, there arise new problems to be dealt with: rising unemployment, precipitous economic decline, and a rising rate of inflation. Inflation can be checked, but only at the price of more unemployment; and if one tries to remedy unemployment, the price is more inflation, which undermines both the national and international economies. In the face of this dilemma, the proponents of a "mixed economy" came up with the idea of using more direct means to control the business cycle, i.e., means such as are used in the state-capitalist countries. Not without some justification, therefore, has this been referred to as "creeping socialism" in capitalist circles, which equate state capitalism with socialism.

State-induced production is also referred to as nationalization, and accordingly state participation in the economy and nationalization of private enterprises give the appearance of being "socialist" measures capable of effecting a fundamental, if slow, transformation of society. As more and more industries are nationalized, the means of production, now state property, would belong to the nation and the market economy would come to an end without revolution. This thought is given further sustenance by the fact that whole industries have, indeed, been nationalized, although in the capitalist market economies where this has taken place, it has so far altered nothing. In the advanced capitalist countries it has for the most part been unprofitable industries or factories which the state has taken over or subsidized, or new enterprises that could only be started with state support and that often gave rise to some intricate concoctions of public and private capital. Still, in these countries private capital remained dominant, the element around which state economic policy turned.

Just as the destruction of capital can contribute to a new upswing by forcing capitalist reorganization, public spending, which rests on unprofitable production, may be seen as a countervailing tendency to capital's own inherent tendency toward disintegration. Capital expansion implies capital destruction; still, every new accumulation phase must surpass the previous one if a renewed upswing is to begin. How long this kind of capitalist reproduction can go on cannot be ascertained a priori from theoretical considerations alone; the answer must await empirical observation once the tendencies working against capitalism's decline show their ultimate ineffectiveness.

Accumulation, which is a necessary condition for a capitalist economy, cannot be replaced by state functions in a "mixed economy." Expanding production alone does not generate profit; for production to yield profit it must take place along with, and in spite of, state-induced production if a state of pseudoprosperity is ever to be overcome in favor of a real boom. If this is no longer possible, sooner or later the crisis-alleviating effect of state-induced production must become blunted and the crisis flare up anew. Any further expansion of state demand would then do no more than add steam to the disintegration of the private sector of the economy, until finally the possibility of any further accumulation would cease to exist. State economic intervention is thus a two-edged sword, and therewith sets its own limits; yet if it stays within these limits, the state of pseudoprosperity it had been able to achieve must ultimately revert to obvious crisis.

A mixed economy is a token of capitalist decay, not a new form of capitalist production relations, as is the case with state capitalism. The dominant position enjoyed by private capital, the indirect methods used to manage the economy, the restriction of state-induced production to public consumption, and the retention of monopolistic competition — all these things together add up to the fact that in a mixed economy the state is still a state of private property which it is the state's task to defend. One cannot expect such a state to make the step from mixed economy to state capitalism on its own; yet without this step it must continue to obey the laws of capitalist production, with no chance of really controlling the economy as required. It can let a crisis run its course, or if surplus values reserves are available, it can try to employ stop-gap measures to keep social unrest at a minimum; but it cannot permanently continue to expand profitless production through inflationary state credits without destroying profit-yielding production in the process.

It is of course true that the economic integration of state and capital cannot be reversed. Private capital had ultimately to call on the services of the state if it was to continue to exist, while the state must rely on private capital in exercising its economic functions. Once effected, integration precludes the state's employing an economic policy contrary to the interests of private capital or its expropriating private capital to thereby assume sole control over the economy. Mixed economies, with or without "socialist" governments, now as in the past are patent proof that in a mixed economy the state still belongs to private capital, which precludes in advance the transition to state capitalism.

It can no longer be maintained that economic management by the state will make for stable capital development or prevent crises; the role of the state, therefore, in a mixed economy is gradually whittled down again to the tasks it has always performed, namely, the use of coercion to maintain existing production relations. With state interventions into the market mechanism ineffective, and the inflated state sector (like the state itself) only a burden accelerating capitalist decline, a mixed economy reverts to commonplace capitalism. The very existence of such a swollen state apparatus requires some cutback in state-induced production (if only to secure the state's own share in the surplus value), and pursuant to this end, the state begins making decisions meant to increase profit and promote accumulation.

At this point the struggle over economic policy sharpens; capital demands an end to all state policies cutting into surplus value, while the victims of these policies call for enlarging the economic powers of the state in the direction of state capitalism. But since state capitalism requires a revolution, that form is not precisely on the order of the day. In the capitalist countries revolutionary Marxism-Leninism is today totally reformist and, moreover, sees itself as such; it has for the time being shelved the goal of state capitalism, not only to protect the existing state-capitalist systems from convulsions but also to meet the ever greater needs of the communist party bureaucrats. Not only, then, is the possibility of state capitalism itself limited by the existing power relations between the classes domestically and among nations worldwide; we even find that state-capitalist principles become adulterated within state capitalism itself and within the "socialist" movements that have cast their lot with it.

State capitalism, clad in the banner of "socialism," appeared to be fundamentally irreconcilable with the capitalist world. But for reasons that we shall not go into here, capitalism was no more able to destroy state capitalism than state capitalism was able to remake the world in its own image. The coexistence of the two systems was a fact long before it was accepted and put to practical advantage by either side. Just as perfect competition has always been but a theoretical construct and has never described capitalism as it really existed, so too is pure state capitalism an abstraction having little to do with historical state capitalism. In either case reality provided only a rough approximation of the features which theory had mapped out in relief, and even these rough approximations varied in appropriateness depending on the broader setting in which the systems were situated. Because state capitalism could not isolate itself from the world market and from world politics, it was deprived from the outset of an intended feature that distinguished it from other systems, namely, economic planning, which, although attempted, remained under the influence of processes taking place in the capitalist world around it. Just as the production "planning" of individual firms stands in sharp contrast to the anarchy reigning in the economy of the capitalist system seen as a whole, under state capitalism national planning takes place within a planless world economy, and its effectiveness is made as questionable on that account as the "rational" efforts of the individual entrepreneur are undermined by the uncontrollable market economy. Thus even state-capitalist nations come under the sway of capitalism's economic cycles, and for this reason they too are interested in maintaining a relative stability on the world market so as not to jeopardize beyond measure their own plan-based economies.

But though there may, indeed, be a general desire for social stability, this is not enough to abolish the laws of motion of capitalist society. The willingness to coexist peaceably alters nothing in the expansion needs of capital and thereby in the imperialistic rivalries between different capitalist systems. The expansion of state capitalism diminishes the expansion of private capital, just as private capital accumulation has an unavoidable influence on planning in the state-capitalist system, and indeed even obliges it to yield to the general need to accumulate. The crisis situation only brings out these contradictions more sharply. Coexistence, therefore, does not mean the integration of the different social systems into one world economy in which all nations participate equally and equitably, but a condition in which existing contradictions have not reached such a critical extreme that they must erupt in violent upheaval. Neither the seemingly "socialist" tendencies of state economic interventions in the capitalist countries nor the capitalist methods and practices of the state-capitalist countries are able to reconcile the two systems and bring about cooperation between the two in their common interest. It has been the temporary possibility of peaceful coexistence, or the temporary impossibility of belligerent confrontations, that has been responsible for the illusion that the economic interests of the two systems could be fulfilled through joint exploitation of the world proletariat.

But joint exploitation is not so much the issue as the dividing up of the ever diminishing loot between the capitals of all descriptions. In this struggle national boundaries are transgressed, and social formations themselves are transcended. The surplus product of the state-capitalist system searches for its enlargement in the surplus value of the capitalist system, while the countries producing surplus value share in the surplus product of state capitalism; the distinction, therefore, between surplus product and surplus value loses all sense and is no longer tenable, at least as far as the world economy as a whole is concerned. While on the one hand the state-capitalist systems, which have undergone their own separate process of integration, are again beginning to show cracks, the common front of capital against state capitalism is also coming apart at the seams. The socialist bloc, envisioned as a second world market, is being engulfed by the capitalist world market, and the political unity of the state-capitalist systems is being undermined in the process.

State capitalism is as little able as capitalism to eliminate national and hence imperialist rivalries. Since no world state exists, the state is tied to the nation and the ruling class is bound to the state. This situation in no way alters either imperialism or the multinational character of many capitalist corporations, since these forms of capitalist internationalism are only means through which certain nationally organized capital entities exercise their power and enlarge their profits. In the state-capitalist nations the national state is the basis on which the new class rules; and state capitalism remains an economy bound to national interests. Were the state-capitalist countries really socialist, they would close ranks and abolish the nation-state both politically and economically. But as things stand now, relations among the state-capitalist countries are essentially the same as those existing in the capitalist world. Common interests must take a back seat to national interests. Differences in political and economic power engender relations of exploitation and dependency, which continue to reproduce themselves without end. Just as in the capitalist camp the stronger powers subordinate the weaker, and though supranational institutions are to be found in both capitalist and state-capitalist countries, the changes they have been able to effect in this regard have been negligible. In the rivalry between capitalist and state-capitalist powers, newly acquired spheres of influence must not only be defended but also expanded. State capitalism itself embarks on an imperialist course in no way inferior to capitalist imperialism except that it avails itself of socialist ideologies. Even this is nothing new, both world wars furnishing prior examples.

Despite their different political and economic forms, capitalism and state capitalism are united in opposition to the interests of the world proletariat. The capital-labor relationship is still the hallmark of all existing production relations. The equation of state ownership with socialism implies no more than the rule of a new class that, in the interests of self-preservation, must close its mind to socialism. The hopes attached to the welfare state of the mixed economy, as well as those engendered by the "socialist" ideology of state capitalism, have been unmasked as illusions by the real development of capital. Although illusions may be dispelled, the conditions that engendered them remain. In both capitalist and state-capitalist countries, the state apparatus can exercise its power without the consent of the workers. But it cannot arrest the decline of capital or eliminate crises, nor can it abolish the class struggle.

The abolition of the "political economy of the workers" in the state-capitalist countries has set the stage for a class struggle that must inevitably turn directly against the state, and which therefore can no longer achieve its more far-reaching socialistic aims within the confines of state capitalism. Even though a mixed economy cannot itself develop into state capitalism, it is still able to use the state to intervene in economic struggles in order to safeguard the continued existence of capital. Indeed, on this account there still exists the danger that the workers will once again limit their political demands to a "workers' state," despite the experiences of the state-capitalist countries, in order to carry the day against their capitalist adversaries. Although for the moment this danger is not acute, it remains implicit in the revolutionary ideologies social democracy and Bolshevism have generated over the past century. If these ideologies continue to prevail in the social struggles we can expect in the future, it is fair to say that the impending revolution already contains the seeds of counterrevolution within it. To abolish capitalism, therefore, the first task is to make Bolshevism a thing of the past once and for all.

1976

6

The Great Depression and the New Deal

Although all capitalistic crises are basically the same, each one varies with respect to its initiation, its length and depth, and the reactions evoked by it. It is the changing capital structure itself which accounts for these variations. Since capitalism is composed of numerous nation-states of dissimilar configurations but operates on a global scale, the international crises affect different countries differently. The economic crisis of 1929 differed from all preceding crises not only in its greater impact on the world economy but also in its political repercussions and their effects on capitalism's further development. It is thus necessary to refer to both the identities and the dissimilarities, as well as to the abstract reasons for and their concrete appearances in any particular crisis, even though all crises are grounded in the capitalist system as such.

The crisis of 1929 came as a great surprise to the Americans. But this was so only because preceding crises had either been forgotten or were referred to as occurences of the irrevocable past, and also because the lack of a general theory of capitalistic development forbade the recognition of the crisis mechanism as the basic "regulator" of the capitalist economy. To be sure, there were business-cycle theories[1] based on empirical evidence. However, they were more of a descriptive than explanatory nature and were generally regarded as aberrations, leaving the rule of standard theory − that is, the theory of the automatic self-adjustability of the market − unaffected. At any rate, the relevant discussions were of a strictly academic character and did not reflect a more general awareness of the contradictions inherent in capitalist production. And this the more so because in principle, as well as for lack of necessary data, there is no way to predict the rise of a crisis that changes a period of prosperity into one of depression. All capitalist actions are, at all times, merely reactions to blindly operating, uncontrollable changes in the socioeconomic relations that underlie the capitalist system and affect it either positively or negatively. However, although a crisis is unpredictable as to the time of its arrival, certain market phenomena indicate its possible approach.

Capitalist prosperity depends on the expansion of capital. Due to the fact of profit production, it is obvious that total social production requires the accumulation of capital to employ the same or an increasing number of workers. Only a part of the total social product falls to the working class; another part serves the consumption needs and the competitively enforced accumulation requirements of the capitalists or capitalist corporations. When the part of the social product earmarked for accumulation is reinvested in additional capital, implying its profitability, there exists a state of prosperity, with a minimum of unemployed labor and the maximum utilization of the means of production. In brief, prosperity depends on the rate of accumulation which, in turn, depends on the given profitability of capital. However, the latter is determined not only by the rate of labor exploitation but also by the mass of profit in relation to the expansion requirements of the already accumulated capital. The same or even an increased rate of exploitation may not suffice to yield a mass of profit conducive to further capital expansion. The consequent arrest or reduction of investments initiates the crisis and the depression in its wake.

There is no need here to dwell on this matter, the less so be-because everyone dealing with it is agreed on the need for capital investments to overcome depressions or to secure a state of prosperity. Whatever the particular depression theory, be it one in terms of overproduction, underconsumption, or market disproportionalities, all recognize the need for the resumption of capital expansion as a precondition for a "normal" economic development and social stability. In practice, at any rate, it is the restoration of a lost profitability that concerns all capitalist reactions to the crisis situation.

Although not recognized as such, the crisis of 1929 was actually a continuation of the unresolved economic crisis preceding

World War I. This crisis had been sidetracked by the war, so to speak, even though the war was itself the political expression of the crisis. The rapid industrialization and capital formation of the Central European powers had demanded a larger share of world exploitation, while the older capitalist nations could only defend their privileged positions through their own continuous expansion, regardless of the capitalization needs of other countries. Since the war was fought for relative shares in world exploitation, it involved all nations either directly or indirectly. Since it ended with the defeat of the Central European countries, it led to a reorganization of the international power structure, with America becoming the leading capitalist nation.

This reorganization affected all European nations negatively – a point not seen at once. For America, however, war production had provided a great impetus for capital expansion, fully justifying President Wilson's anticipations when, in 1916, he told his fellow-citizens that "we must play a great part in the world whether we choose it or not. We have got to finance the world in some important degree and those who finance the world must understand it and rule it with their spirits and their minds."[2] The temporary eclipse of European competition gave the United States a foothold on formerly inaccessible shores, and the anarchic conditions of devastated Europe helped to secure the newly won positions. America turned from a debtor into a creditor nation, and her rise to economic dominance changed all existing international relations.

America's postwar prosperity was based on a productive apparatus built to support a worldwide war. The accelerated capital expansion had enough momentum to continue long beyond the existence of the conditions that had been its cause. But finally America, too, succumbed to the postwar realities, and her expansion came to a halt in 1929, not again to be resumed on any significant scale until World War II. The Great Depression had its "start" in America only because in other countries the postwar depression had never really ended. But the American collapse led these nations into even deeper decline and disorganized trade relations almost to the point of extinction. There was no profit in further expansion, and there was no way to organize the economic world structure in accordance with the profit requirements of a general resumption of the accumulation process.

Prior to 1929 depressions were of a deflationary nature, that is, the "laws of the market" were allowed to run their course, in the expectation that sooner or later the supply and demand mechanism would regain a lost equilibrium, restore the profitability of capital, and thus assure its further development. The war economy itself, however, was an inflationary process, as the increasing indebtedness of governments pressed upon the profitability of capital. The increased production had been for "public consumption," destroying men, materials, and machines and delaying the production of the profitable means of production on which the expansion of capital depends.

In a "purely" economic depression the deflationary process merely destroys capital values, through bankruptcies and lowered prices, without seriously affecting their physical counterparts, the means of production. The resulting shift of value relations – that is, the changed distribution of the socially available profit among the capitalist firms – will in time provide the surviving capital entities with a higher rate of profit and thus with incentives for new investments. The capitalistic concentration and centralization process plays a greater mass of profit into the hands of fewer capitals, thereby improving their chances to resume their expansion on the basis of an altered capital structure, which allows for an increase in the productivity of labor and a profitable accumulation. The destruction of capital values during an ordinary depression is thus a precondition for a new economic upswing, which is to say that the deflationary process is an indispensable requirement of capital development.

The war economy, however, is of an inflationary nature. Capital values are sustained in the form of the public debt. The postwar depression of the European economies was thus characterized by monetary inflation in order to eliminate the public debt and to change the distribution of the social product in favor of capital. The inflationary measures varied in different countries in accordance with both their economic health and their monetary policies. The victor nations attempted, at first, to restore the international gold standard suspended during the war in order to maintain, or

renew, their prewar positions in the international credit and investment markets. But the recovery of the European economies was
far too slow to achieve social stability and a level of economic
activity sufficient to promote another period of general expansion.
In contrast, and after a short-lived depression in 1921, the American economy prospered to an extent unknown at any other time.
Prices remained relatively stable, profits increased, the labor force
expanded, and the new inventions — automobiles, telephones,
radios, refrigerators, etc. — found continually expanding markets.

However, for both internal and external reasons the American
prosperity could not last. Although America's dependence on foreign trade is less than that of other capitalist countries, it is there
nonetheless, as the expansion of capital implies the extension of
markets through capital and commodity exports. This, of course,
requires the ability of other nations to buy American goods, that
is, their own ability to sell on the American market. But the war
and the ensuing European stagnation had led to a further disintegration of foreign trade, which was already greatly hampered by
protectionist policies and important differentials in labor productivity. Though not immediately perceivable, the sad state of the
European economies was bound to affect America's prosperity,
for, just as every major crisis arising somewhere spreads over the
whole globe, so a state of prosperity cannot be maintained in isolation from the rest of the world.

Assuming capitalism were a closed system, it would reach its
limits at that point of development where the number of workers
and their productivity — as determined by the accumulation of
capital — would not yield profits large enough for its further expansion. At such a point accumulation, and therewith the system
itself, would come to a halt. The fact of continuous accumulation
in the real capitalist world shows that these abstract limits have
not been reached, while the recurrent crises indicate the existence
of these limits, which come concretely to light in the interruptions
of the expansion process. It is then a question of adjusting the
profitability of capital to its expansion requirements which determines the state of the economy. As long as these adjustments can
be made in the sphere of production, via the market relations, it
is possible, although not certain, to overcome the immanent bar-

riers to the production of capital. With respect to the American prosperity that preceded the crash of 1929, the emerging discrepancy between the possible rate of labor exploitation and the objectively required rate of expansion necessary to sustain the conditions of prosperity showed itself in the increasingly speculative character of this prosperity and in the enormous expansion of the credit system.

The American prosperity was largely and increasingly based on fictitious profits and fictitious capital, "created" on the stock market, which had no equivalent in real capital values and real profits. To some extent these fictitious values and their continuous expansion functioned just the same as an impetus for the further increase of production, even though this increase was not based on actual but on expected profits, which might or might not be realized. The increase in production, in turn, accelerated the speculative fever made possible through the availability of bank credits. Because from a capitalistic point of view it is quite immaterial for what particular purposes credits are extended, they will be used where they are the most lucrative. At the same time, however, credit expansion indicates a shortage of capital for the maintenance of a given pace of capital expansion. While credit itself can create nothing, it may prolong, or initiate, a scale of production that would have been far lower without it. It is for this reason that every crisis of capital is preceded by an extraordinary credit increase, by an effort, that is, to expand the level of production in order to maintain a given rate of profit. As the harbinger of an approaching crisis, the credit extension is also instrumental in the rapidity of the economic collapse, when production fails to reach a level of profitability commensurable with the blown-up mass of capital. In any case profits can only be made through production; and if they are not satisfactory with respect to the existing capital, whether real or fictitious, the claims based on them cannot be met and a part of the recognized capital ceases to be such.

Although initiated by the stock market crash of 1929, the ensuing depression was not the result of mere speculation or of a false monetary policy promoting credit extension for speculative purposes. Both occurrences fell together with a slackening of the rate of investment due to declining profits in relation to the employed capital. It was rather this situation, the relative stagnation of productive capital, which led to the speculative boom, which could only enlarge the overall discrepancy between the profitability and the expansionary needs of the economy. Even without the artificial expansion of the market value of capital, the upswing was bound to come to an end, although, perhaps, this might have happened at some other time, with less dramatic impact and fewer disastrous consequences than those released by the stock market collapse and the disintegration of the banking system.

As it was, however, the crisis was blamed on the stock market, that is, on the unexplained loss of nerve at the first serious decline of the selling boom, which lowered or wiped out not only the inflated part of stock values but also part of the "justified" market value of capital. Treated as a question of psychology, all that seemed necessary in this situation was to halt the decline of stock prices by the restoration of confidence in the workability and progressive unfolding of the system. But since "confidence" cannot replace money, the capitalists tried first of all to safeguard as much as possible of the money value of their stock by selling at any price, so long as buyers could be found. In a short time the stock market value of capital was reduced to half the size it had reached in 1929, leading to the collapse of many enterprises and financial institutions. Banks began to fail because their loans had served speculation instead of productive investments, and their failures led to runs on the banks for reasons both of fear and of necessity.

The productive apparatus of the nation was not affected by these happenings in its financial structure. The reduction of the market value of capital, as registered on the stock market, should have improved the profitability of industrial production, since it could now be related to a diminished mass of capital. The fact, however, that production declined even further demonstrated that the cause of the crisis was not to be found in the speculative boom but was rather the result of an already existing decline of the economy. This showed itself most drastically in agriculture, where prices had fallen to about half of their war-time height, not to rise throughout the 1920s. Industrial workers, as a whole, were not able during this period to reach what was officially considered the necessary annual minimum wage of $2,000. Though the demand for labor increased, it did not increase fast enough to offset the declining rate of capital expansion which, due to the rising productivity of labor, accompanied an increase of output of about 40 percent. But this was in the main output of consumer goods not destined for the expansion of capital-producing capital. That the existing rate of growth could still be regarded as a prosperous one was precisely due to the frozen wage level and the decline of farm prices, which bolstered the profitability of industrial capital and restricted the prosperity to a privileged minority. According to estimates of the Brookings Institution, "in the boom year of 1929, 78 percent of all American families had incomes of less than $3,000. Forty percent had family incomes of less than $1,500. Only 2.3 percent of the population enjoyed incomes of over $10,000. Sixty thousand American families, in the highest income brackets, held savings which amounted to the total held by the bottom 25 million families."[3]

In the bourgeois view all production is destined for consumption and therefore determined by the consumers. Actually production is determined by its profitability. Its aim is the transformation of a given capital into a larger one, which can only be realized at the expense of consumption. If consumption were the rationale of production, there would be no accumulation of capital. There might be an expansion of the productive apparatus as a precondition for the expansion of consumption, but not the accumulation of capital as capital. No matter what a capitalist firm or corporation produces, it will always try for the largest difference between its production costs and the selling prices for its commodities. On the social level this implies that there is always a surplus product that does not enter into consumption but takes on the form of additional capital, unless it remains idle money capital. In the latter form, however, it can only comprise a fraction of the total of the unused capital, which finds its augmentation in idle production capacity, unsalable inventories, and a general glut on the commodity markets. With production frozen in the commodity form and unable to take on the money form, the capitalist crisis also manifests itself as an interruption of the circulation process and a general shortage of money. That is to say, the idle money, which cannot find profitable employment, comes to the fore as a general lack of money and a decreasing effective demand. And thus it seems that the crisis is caused by overproduction or its corollary, insufficient demand, whereas, actually, these are only market manifestations of an interrupted process of accumulation.

It is not enough, then, to enlarge the output of consumer goods, as happened during America's postwar prosperity, unless the larger output is accompanied by a corresponding extension of the productive apparatus through which the expansion of capital is materialized. The increase of consumer goods may be a consequence of accumulation, but it cannot be its source, since it depresses the profitability of capital by reducing the rate of accumulation. It was thus the boom in consumer durables, under conditions of relative capital stagnation, which provided one of the contradictions of the prosperity. Of course, this was not a question of economic policy but an expression of blocked investment opportunities due to the precarious conditions of the world economy. The rate of capital expansion depends on the mass of profit available after social consumption needs have been met. The less consumed, the more can be accumulated, and vice versa. But in the world at large production scarcely sufficed to assure the necessary consumption requirements, and profit rates were consequently low. It was the low rate of profit which prevented American capital exports through direct investments abroad. What capital export there was took the form of short-term credits, which could not be transformed into long-term investments. In fact, a great part of this capital returned to the United States via the reparation and allied-debt arrangements. While America financed the German reparations, the latter financed the allied war-time debt to the United States. This circular money flow could not enhance a general upswing and came to an end before capital stagnation turned into the Great Depression.

Of interest in this context was America's inability to expand its capital either internally or externally. Still, money had been made during the war, and was being made after it, to allow for a buying boom suggestive of a real prosperity, even though it was not based on the expansion of capital. But this could only be a temporary affair, not only because it was so largely based on credit, but also because profits did not rise with the increasing economic activity. It was a period often dubbed in retrospect a "profitless prosperity," which offered no incentives for further capital investments. Not only was the existing productive capacity able to accommodate the prevailing demand, but it was never fully used throughout this whole period. Production did not exceed the demand formed by consumption goods and was, by that token, capitalistically unjustifiable. There was no overproduction as yet because production had been curtailed to the given market demand, which did not include sufficient demand for new plants and equipment.

Socially this implied capital stagnation, which denies a part of capital, namely that part producing for expansion, its necessary profits, thereby reducing the general rate of profit for capital as a whole. To raise the rate of profit, as a precondition for the enlargement of capital, requires a restructuring of the whole of the economy, which leads to the profitability of a still larger mass of the total capital. To this end the reallocation of the social capital in a market economy is only possible by way of crises and depressions. But the crisis must first make its appearance on the surface of the market, even though it was already present in changed value relations in the production process. And it is via the market that the needed reorganization of the capital structure is brought about, even though this must be actualized through changes in the exploitative capital-labor relations at the point of production.

Before this happens the depression runs its course. After the stock market collapse production declined progressively, reducing the national income within three years to less than half of what it was in 1929. Apart from enterprises disappearing altogether, production was generally cut, which led by 1932 to 15 million unemployed. Many of the employed workers were on half-time. To give a particular instance, industrial construction, which is an indicator for general production, declined from $949 million to $74 million; steel production was down to 12 percent of its capacity. Five thousand banks closed, wiping out close to 10 million savings accounts. Farm income, which amounted in 1929 to $12 billion, was reduced by 1932 to $5 billion. The price of crude oil, which had been $2.31 per barrel in 1926, fell to 10 cents by the end of 1930.

This list could be continued endlessly, for the crisis was all-inclusive and, with the exception of the really rich, affected all layers of society.

It was perhaps the very rapidity of the decline which stunned the population into a kind of disbelief in the reality of the crisis. This situation could not possibly last, it was thought, and would end as suddenly as it had come about. As in a natural catastrophe, all tried to rescue what was still savable; the entrepreneurs by cut-throat competition, the workers by accepting lower wages. The government of Herbert Hoover ceaselessly assured the population that the depression would end in a few weeks, that it had nothing to do with the economic system, which was basically as sound as ever, but was probably caused by unsound speculation activities on the part of other nations and unfair terms of trade. As the depression persisted, a false optimism took the place of despair, for it was now said "that the slump has continued so long and has proceeded so far that it seems hardly tenable to believe that the end is still far off. It is on this idea. . . that a spirit of optimism is growing up in business circles."[4] To improve upon this new optimism, reductions in the higher income tax rates were proposed in order to induce new capital investments, in the belief that additional capital expenditures would raise the national income and finally yield larger revenues at the lower tax rate. Public works were initiated to reduce unemployment, but within the frame of a balanced budget. Eventually, however, taxes were raised in the interest of "sound finance," because "the first requirement of confidence and of economic recovery is the financial stability of the United States government, and because government borrowings would denude commerce and industry of their resources, jeopardize the financial system, and actually extend unemployment and demoralize agriculture rather than relieve it."[5] The measures taken to counteract the depression, or rather the lack of such measures, intensified the crisis but did not diminish Hoover's optimism, for, as he later explained, "it is the function of Presidents to be encouraging," even when this contradicts the facts.

The highly unequal distribution of income that characterizes the capitalistic upswing and is, in fact, its precondition, becomes even more unequal in times of depression. A part of the lower incomes disappears altogether, while another part is severely curtailed; and this reduction of buying power is euphemistically described as a lack of "effective demand," causing the general overproduction. Of course, since the economy does not come to a dead stop, part of production continues to yield wages and profits, and their recipients find themselves in an enviable position, which they try to maintain with all the means at their disposal. The social misery is not at once a general misery, and this divides the privileged from the unfortunates even more than before, each group fearing the other, which intensifies the conflicts between classes and within the various layers of society.

For some time, however, the population at large seemed to share Hoover's confidence in the viability of the economic system, for the complaints made were directed not so much against the system as such as against its mismanagement by an incompetent government. The latter was expected to restore the customary conditions of the past, not alter the social structure. In the absence of an effectively organized counterideology, the capitalist ideology maintained its hold over the broad masses, which desired the end of the depression, not the end of capitalism. It was this mental climate which explains the rather curious first reactions to the deepening depression, namely, the various self-help schemes, which occupied great numbers of people, either by a return to the land, where this seemed feasible, or by all sorts of barter agreements based on diverse kinds of labor. These were of course no solutions but makeshift arrangements to weather the depression, the ending of which was presumably the work of the government, or of a new government should the existing one fail in this.

However, the depression is no respecter of ideology, and necessity immunizes against all false consciousness. Whatever the conformist notions of the dispossessed and unemployed, they had to eat; and without any savings to speak of, they had to rely on charity in order to exist. There was no unemployment insurance, no relief program for the destitute millions, only private charity and communal welfare institutions hardly able to deal with the ever present social misery and totally unfit to deal with mass unemployment. Yet there were no other places people could turn for help. Streaming into the welfare agencies, they soon found a way to act collectively by spontaneously forming loose organizations based on the locations of these agencies.

During the first three years of the depression, no real efforts were made to adapt the relief institutions to the demands of the crisis. An ineffective public works program was soon abandoned. It was a principle on the part of the government that the crisis should be met through "the maintenance of a spirit of mutual self-help through voluntary giving. This is of infinite importance to the future of America. No governmental action, no economic doctrine, no economic plan or project can replace that God-imposed responsibility of the individual man and woman to their neighbors."[6] But the number of neighbors able or willing to help decreased even more rapidly than the number of unemployed increased. The state governments had to come to the rescue of the local communities, until state funds, too, were exhausted, leaving the Federal Government as the last resort.

The depression went deeper and deeper, leading to a social crisis that could be overcome only by way of a sharp policy turn and the government's conscious intrusion into the economic system. By the end of 1932 the politicians, and some economists, were increasingly prone to express fearful prophecies to the effect that if a satisfactory solution of the unemployment problem were not found soon, great convulsions and hunger riots would be unavoidable. A noticeable radicalization of the jobless as well as the employed showed itself in hunger marches, while spontaneous demonstrations and even plundering became increasingly frequent. More organizations of the unemployed came into being on their own or were formed with the aid of existing political labor organizations. The unrest became an object of great concern, since it expressed itself in an atmosphere of general uncertainty and social tension. In and of itself the unemployed movement was too weak to pass the bounds in which it could be held down with the usual instrumentalities, but in conjunction with the state of mind prevailing throughout society, it formed the seat of a general fermentation which, at times, was assuming an almost revolutionary character.

The gradual exhaustion of the sources of relief implied increasing misery. The minimum amount by which starvation could be warded off was at the time 22 cents daily per person, but no-where could this amount be raised. Rents, like bills for light and cooking gas, could not be paid, and people were evicted from their homes. The extremely low standard of living caused the rate of ill-ness to shoot upward, with dysentery and pellagra the dominating diseases. Crime was for many the only means of existence. The dis-tress of the homeless became ever more acute. On the edge of the cities the unemployed built for themselves so-called Hoovervilles out of boxes, tin cans, and the refuse of dumps; holes in the earth used as dwelling places ceased to be a rarity. Thousands upon thousands lived in improvised tent camps. People by the millions roamed the highways, moving from the north and the east to the south and the west to get away from the housing problem and also in the false hope of finding some way to exist elsewhere. Driven out by force from hostile communities, they lived in "jungles," in railway cars, and under bridges. Breadlines were overcrowded and people were freezing to death in the cold. Still, rebellions were only sporadic and were suppressed with the utmost brutality. The great despair created an even greater fear on the part of the au-thorities, which prepared the police and National Guard for civil war. The army itself was called upon to defeat the veterans of World War I, who demonstrated in Washington to demand early payment of a promised bonus, only to be dispersed with the aid of cannon, tanks, machine guns, and flame throwers under the com-mand of MacArthur and Eisenhower.

The real responsibility for this misery, according to John Edgerton of the National Association of Manufacturers, lay with the jobless themselves, for "they do not practice the habit of thrift and conservation, but gamble away their savings in the stock mar-ket and elsewhere. Why blame our economic system, or govern-ment, or industry?"[7] While this attitude is understandable, it is also meaningless, since it does not remove the problem of per-sistent mass unemployment and its possible social consequences. What is more astonishing was the refusal on the part of the impov-erished to make themselves responsible for the elimination of their misery. Instead, they insisted on the "right to work" and de-manded from the government the means of existence until the de-mand had been met. Even where they directly violated private property — for instance, by taking possession of unused mines to dig coal to be sold on the market on their own account — they invoked the principle of necessity, not the conviction that capitalism had become untenable.

Whatever the numerous reasons why the American workers did not possess that degree of class consciousness which characterized the workers in the industrial European nations, "the overriding, central fact was that during the worst and longest depression in the history of any industrial nation the American working class did not show any demonstrable change in its political and economic commitments."[8] And though that degree of class consciousness displayed in Europe led nowhere, it at least provided some independent response to the economic crisis, whereas in America the movements of protest addressed themselves exclusively to the as yet unchallenged social institutions. Quite apart from the question as to whether the left-wing political organizations were prepared for any anticapitalist actions, should a chance have offered itself, they were at any rate programmatically committed to some type of social change. But in the elections of 1932, the Socialists received fewer votes than they had received thirty years before, and the Communists polled only 120,000 votes.

Generally hope was associated with a new government, one more willing to combat the depression than was possible under the basically deflationary policies of the Hoover administration. These policies had already been breached by force of circumstances. Some government aid was dispensed via the creation of the Reconstruction Finance Corporation in 1931, which was authorized to lend money to banks, businesses, and farms to shore up the faltering economy. Public works to help both private business and the unemployed led to large deficits, despite the desire for a balanced budget. But the decline continued and found no adequate compensatory reactions through government. As the economic system was not challenged, it was the Hoover administration which had to take the blame for the unmitigated distress. The two-party system of American politics automatically ensured that the Democratic Party should gain from the failures of the Republican administration. The 1932 elections brought the Democrats into power and Franklin D. Roosevelt into the White House. In his preelection speeches, as is customary, Roosevelt promised everything to everybody but, in however a general way, insisted on the government's responsibility to strengthen the economy and to aid its casualties. He promised a government committed to pulling the nation out of the depression, in contrast to Hoover, for whom such ideas implied the subjugation of economic laws to the arbitrary rule of government and the destruction of traditional capitalism.

Roosevelt had no such intentions. What his ambition desired was the presidency, and to get himself elected he did not hesitate to propose incompatible solutions to the social problems. He, too, was for a balanced budget and, at the same time, for government interventions in the economy on behalf of the general welfare. "Through his warm, outgoing approach and his setting forth of generalities, he had kept a heavy majority in Congress and among the public behind him. They read into his promises their own wishes. . . . In the twentieth-century tradition, he was trying very hard to be President of all the American people. . . . To the desperate Americans of 1933, Roosevelt wished to dispense aid to all groups — but, and here was where much trouble began, to require concessions and responsibilities from each in return. As Roosevelt had to make choices and move from generalities to specifics, misunderstandings developed and disappointments burgeoned. These came later. In that first summer the New Deal seemed to encompass businessmen, farmers, workers; men and women; the white-collared and the blue-collared — all in the alliance for recovery."[9]

Roosevelt's party slogan, the New Deal, implied the beginning of a fresh game but with the same players. The old cardsharps were to be turned into honest men, sacrificing their advantages so as not to ruin their partners and the game. Class collaboration and fair competition, the unattainable ideals of bourgeois society, were finally to be realized through the neutral umpireship of a benevolent government. The impossible was to be made possible by an act of will to see society prosper again as it had at times in the past. But how to begin? As always by dealing with the material nearest at hand. It was the very lack of a definite program, the playful experimentation with concrete issues, the pragmatic approach of learning by doing which overcame the downward trend of stagnation and the general apathy to which it had led.

Roosevelt's inauguration coincided with what was perhaps the lowest point of the depression. In his inaugural address Roosevelt insisted that the nation must now move "as a trained and loyal army willing to sacrifice for the good of a common discipline." To that end he would demand from Congress "the one remaining instrument to meet the crisis — a broad Executive power to wage war against the emergency, as great as the power that would be given to me if we were in fact invaded by a foreign foe."[10] His first presidential actions were then aptly described as the "hundred-days war." It began with an attack on the financial chaos through the declaration of a bank holiday to stem withdrawals from the banks that were still functioning. Those banks which appeared to be solvent were reopened under guarantees of the government. The Emergency Banking Act authorized the Federal Reserve System to provide its members with practically unlimited credits. The run on the banks was actually halted, and in order not to lose the newly gained confidence in the restored banking system, the Federal Deposit Insurance System was established by law, insuring small depositors against future losses.

Aware of the fact that only inflationary methods could block a further decline of the economy, Roosevelt still searched for a type of inflation that would not unduly enlarge the national debt. He tried, on the one hand, to reduce the costs of government and, on the other, to increase the money supply through the issuing of unsecured currency and through the devaluation of the dollar. Since other countries, including Great Britain, had left the gold standard in the fall of 1931, devaluation of the dollar had been expected also in the United States, and the dollar, and with it gold, was leaving the country. To halt the flight of the dollar, as well as to devaluate it, Rosevelt suspended the convertibility of the dollar into gold for American citizens and temporarily stopped the export of gold. He then devaluated the dollar in terms of gold by 40 percent. America left the gold standard. The devaluation raised prices to some extent and provided the monetary means to finance the recovery program. Roosevelt liked to think of these measures not so much as inflationary but as the application of the principle of "monetary management."

Legislation followed in quick succession to deal with the ag-

ricultural crisis, unemployment, and the economy in general. The
Agricultural Adjustment Administration saw its main function in
the raising of farm prices through crop reductions. The farmers'
plight was caused not only by the lack of demand for their products but also by a disparity between agricultural and industrial
prices due to the more advanced monopolization of industry. Numerous farmers could no longer pay their taxes, not to speak of
the interests on their mortgages, and faced dispossession from
their farms, which they often succeeded in preventing by direct
action. There was seemingly a greater militancy in the rural than in
the urban population, no doubt because in the farmers' case property was directly involved. Credit was extended to them in return
for their reduction of production. Since American agriculture is almost exclusively based on single cash crops, a change to subsistence
farming was not feasible; hunger stalked the countryside as well as
the city slums. It is a curious situation, indeed, when a general
abundance of foodstuffs finds its accompaniment in starvation,
even among the food producers, and when no other solution offers
itself but the reduction of production and the destruction of unsalable food products. It is just as curious to speak of overproduction when, in fact, food is merely withheld from people more than
ready to consume it. Yet foodstuffs of all descriptions were
dumped and covered with poison and quicklime to prevent the
hungry from using it. Wheat and cotton were plowed under, millions of pigs and cows were destroyed in the hope of raising prices,
through artificial scarcities. Farmers were rewarded for not producing commodities, although this was of benefit only to the larger
agricultural enterprises, not to the small farmers.

Like anything else in the New Deal, its agricultural program
was beset with many contradictions. A false romanticism on the
part of Roosevelt was able to combine the reduction of agricultural production with the desire to lead at least part of the superfluous city population back to the serenity of country life. The
drift from the land to the city in search for more lucrative occupa-
tions, or any kind of work, was to be reversed by a government-
sponsored homestead policy as a part of the solution of the farm
problem. While the number of farmers was to be increased, or at
least maintained, production was to be reduced in order to raise

prices to provide a living for all. But crop limitation allowed the landlords to drive their tenant farmers from the land and at the same time to pocket their share of government subsidies. "Recovery" of this type merely increased the misery of tenants and sharecroppers. But, then, they were an inarticulate and powerless minority, which could easily be overlooked even among the "forgotten men."

Like all good Americans, Roosevelt hated the English "dole," into which a limited system of unemployment insurance had "degenerated," providing direct cash relief without work. An inescapable change from relief in kind to cash relief threatened to bring the "dole" to America. This morale-destroying situation could only be prevented by the combination of relief with work, which characterized the whole unemployment program under the New Deal. The early Civil Works Administration (CWA) invented work for "work's sake" to give regular exercise and training to the workers, so that they would be in good condition when business might need them back. "The fact that enormous numbers of people were getting out of the habit of working," it was said, "together with the impossibility of getting the young ones into the habit, aroused the greatest concern among those responsible for the framing of social policy. The old stigma of idleness must be re-established, that stigma which gave this country its development, until a rising offer of work may meet with an eager acceptance at least."[11] The young, in particular, had to be rescued from the disintegrating influence of the combination of idleness and want. To that end the Civil Conservation Corps (CCC) came into being to put the 18- to 25-year-old men into labor camps and to occupy them, in exchange for room, board, and some pocket money, with the planting of trees, the building of minor roads, tracks, and dams, and the fight against soil erosion. Although the CCC form of relief was the most expensive, it was the only one that found general appreciation, for as its director, R. Fechner, pointed out, "the 2,300,000 youths trained in CCC camps since its inception in March 1933, were about 85 percent prepared for military life and could be turned into first-class fighting men at almost an instant's notice."[12]

At the same time, public works were resumed under Harold

L. Ickes of the Public Works Administration (PWA) in order to combine the reduction of unemployment with the stimulation of capital expenditures, but with only minor results in either direction. City halls, courthouses, schools, post offices, highways, and harbors were constructed, but with so much caution that it was hardly possible to speak of an increase of public works. Rather, "they have merely been prevented from fading altogether. Public works, as such, in fact, have played only a relatively small part in the experimentation of 'deficit financing' by which it was hoped 'to prime the pump' of recovery."[13]

The costs of work relief are far higher than those of direct relief. At the beginning of 1934 the Civil Works Administration had more than four million persons on its payroll, some of whom were not eligible for public welfare. The large expense induced Roosevelt to put an end to the CWA and to return its clients to the relief rolls, which cut government expenses by more than half and subjected the relief recipients once again to the humiliations of the "means test," that is, the proof of total destitution. A year later, however, Roosevelt found it necessary to reinstitute public employment and to launch the Works Progress Administration (WPA), which hired about three million people out of more than twenty million relief recipients. The WPA paid somewhat more than was allotted to welfare cases, but less than the prevailing wage rates, so as not to "encourage the rejection of opportunities for private employment."

The sudden changes in welfare policy led to serious flare-ups among the unemployed and to attempts, with the aid of the left-wing political organizations, to form a nationally coordinated movement that could act as a pressure group in Congress and influence events in the interests of the unemployed. But their lobbying activities were of little avail. More disturbing in the eyes of Roosevelt and the "progressive" wing of the Democratic Party was the spreading of competitive "fascist" tendencies, as exemplified by the rise and growing power of Huey Long in Louisiana, who took some of the wind out of Roosevelt's sails by a more consistent demagoguery, which did not hesitate to promise a thorough distribution of wealth that would make "every man a king." All kinds of schemes for resolving the economic crisis were advanced, such as the so-called Townsend Plan, or Old-Age Pension Program, and Upton Sinclair's "End Poverty in California" plan, which was to give the workers some access to the means of production and distribute the wealth more evenly. These movements intensified a divisive ideological split within the Democratic Party and drove its "conservative" wing to the Republicans in opposition to the New Deal. To keep the party intact and to retain its leadership, Roosevelt tried to balance the contrary interests by means of compromises, which either advanced or retarded the New Deal. The frictions in the Democratic Party reflected those within the nation as a whole and explain the increasingly visible partisanship as well as opposition with respect to the New Deal measures.

The Grand Design of the New Deal, namely, the National Industrial Recovery Act (NRA), was thus destined to fall apart without, and independently of, the fact that the Supreme Court of the United States declared it in violation of the Constitution and therefore invalid, together with the AAA and some other New Deal legislation. The NRA implied business self-regulation, under the auspices of government, to end the state of fierce competition that brought prices and wages down without reaching a new stabilizing economic plateau. It indicated the loss of confidence in the self-adjustability of the market mechanism. "The cat is out of the bag," wrote R. G. Tugwell, one of Roosevelt's early advisers, "there is no invisible hand. There never was. We must now supply a real and visible guiding hand to do the task which that mythical, nonexisting, invisible agency was supposed to perform, but never did."[14] The economy had to be planned in order to remain a capitalist economy. It is therefore no contradiction that the "planning" consisted exactly of those measures that had hitherto been the results of unconscious market forces, that is, the increasing concentration of capital and its acceleration in times of crisis and depression. To facilitate this process, antitrust laws had to be set aside to allow trade associations to fix their own prices and profit margins through a "fair" distribution of market shares in all industries.

Harking back to the "unifying" experiences of World War I, during which the government was to some extent able to subordinate all special interests to the "common" goal of winning the war, the "war" on the depression was supposed to yield similar results through the suspension of capital competition and the elimination of class conflicts. The self-regulation of business was therefore to be complemented by strengthening organized labor to assure more equal working conditions and to uphold "reasonable" wage levels. Parallel to setting behavioral codes for the various industries, the NRA, through special legislation, was to guarantee the workers' right to collective bargaining and the unhampered formation of independent trade unions. And this the more so because in 1932 the American labor movement showed signs of a revived militancy both despite and because of its organizational decay. Union membership, which comprised about 12 percent of all employed workers in 1922, had been decimated to 6 percent by 1932. From then on, however, the number of strikes to defend both wages and unions increased rapidly, which merely led to a further deterioration of the economy. The argument for the labor clause of the NRA was based on the consideration "that unions tended to keep wages up, hours down and working conditions safe — all purposes of the plan. The most cutthroat competition, worsening all three, invariably came from those industries or low-cost areas that kept unions out. The pattern in the steel industry or much of the South was that anyone who joined a union lost his job. If such industries or areas were to have the benefit of the codes, then their workers should be allowed to join unions and bargain collectively."[15]

For lack of any comprehension of the contradictions inherent in capital production, Roosevelt and the proponents of the New Deal were "underconsumptionists," that is, they mistook the results of the depression for its cause. Wages were to be propped up to increase the buying power for a larger production, and prices were to rise with higher wages, thereby increasing the entrepreneurial profits. It was all so simple; it only ignored the fact that wages are costs of production, so that the higher they are, the lower will be profits and the incentive for production increases. When prices are raised, the buying power of wages is cut down, of course, unless wages and profits rise at the same time, which presupposes capital expansion under conditions of full employment. But for the advocates of the New Deal, depression meant lowered wages and declining prices, and raising both was then the way to recovery. This was to be attained through the restraint of competition, without regard for the actual profitability of capital, on which the state of the economy, and therewith the state of competition, depends. Monopolization, being the effect of competition, was now to be reached without competition, by means of gentlemen's agreements that assured everyone the required profits and the workers a living wage.

In reality things worked out quite differently, or rather they worked out in the only way they could within the confines of capitalism. Although most industries subscribed to NRA codes, or at least paid lip service to them, the codes were written up, and the authorities therewith created were dominated by big business and its special interests to the detriment of small producers, the workers, and the public at large. The control over prices and production granted to the various trade associations reduced itself finally to mere price fixing, which broke the deflationary spiral but did not enhance the economy to any noticeable extent. It did, however, accentuate the further concentration of capital and, in that sense, was one of the preconditions for the resumption of the capital-expansion process. The unlamented demise of the NRA by verdict of the Supreme Court led to some shadowboxing on the part of Roosevelt, although it merely removed the legal sanction from the "natural" course of events, namely, the increasing monopolization of capital.

What has been said so far does not exhaust the measures taken under the New Deal. But what has been left out are its relatively minor aspects, such as the often-repeated attempted reform of the security markets in order to reduce fraudulent speculation; some restriction of banking practices to protect deposits; workmen's accident compensation laws; employment agencies to expedite the allocation of labor; and the government's entry into the power business, through the Tennessee Valley Authority, which was supposed to serve as a "yardstick" to evaluate the pricing policies of private power companies and to reclaim wasteland through the erection of dams and waterways. Long overdue innovations, such as the Social Security Act, involving unemployment and old-age insurance, and the National Labor Relations Act, became laws in the middle of 1935.

Within the context of the outspokenly reactionary character of American capitalism, all this New Deal legislation appeared to be of a progressive nature, challenging the tradition of "rugged individualism" and comforting those who saw themselves as "collectivists" merely because they opposed strict laissez faire in favor of social reforms such as had long been realized in the European capitalist nations. While the bourgeois reform movement was based on the fear of the possible consequences of the increasing polarization of society and its effect on the class struggle, the workers took advantage of the temporary division of the ruling class to attend to their own immediate needs. The growing capitalist opposition to the New Deal forced the Roosevelt administration to rely to some extent on the good will and the support of the working class, if only to save the capitalist system from the folly of its less-enlightened defenders. The labor clause of the NRA, legally defining the right to organize, encouraged the extension of old organizations and the formation of new ones, but it also induced the capitalists to fight these organizations and their demands despite the NRA. The passing of the National Labor Relations Act created the impression that the government was solidly behind labor's organization drive and would compel industry to accept its results. Roosevelt became the hero and defender of the working class.

With the government seemingly on the side of labor, a strike wave ensued for higher wages and better working conditions, based on the reviving trade unions and newly formed industrial unions, represented by the CIO. The fight for union recognition embraced industries such as steel, rubber, textiles, automobiles, which had until then managed to keep unions out. Unionization took on spectacular proportions, with often a tenfold increase in membership within one year. The resistance of management gave these struggles a militant character, with − for America − new tactics, such as the sit-down strike and even, as in San Francisco, the general strike. The government's noninterference brought Roosevelt much of the labor vote in 1936 as well as heavy financial support in the election campaign. But with the main industries organized and the unions bureaucratized, rank-and-file initiative again subsided to make room for the ordinary bargaining procedures of the labor market, thus revealing the hollowness of labor's victories, which had only served to integrate the unions more thoroughly into the capitalist system.

Working-class militancy also reflected a changing economic situation, noticeable not only in America but on a worldwide scale. The downward trend had been arrested. The forces of recovery operating within the depression, as well as the decrease in unemployment via public expenditures, increased production up to the output level of 1929. This was sufficient for the Roosevelt administration to drastically reduce public works, as well as the WPA, in a new effort to balance the budget in response to the demands of the business world. But the output level of 1929 had not been enough to avoid a large amount of unemployment. "We must look to a much more rapid expansion of production than has taken place between 1933 and 1935," wrote David Weintraub, "before we can expect a return either to the unemployment or the employment levels of the pre-depression period. A rough calculation indicates that, in order for unemployment to drop to the 1929 level by 1937, goods and services produced would have to reach a point 20 percent higher than that of 1929, even if the productivity level of 1935 remained unchanged."16 However, it was the restoration of profitability on the existing level of production, not full employment, which motivated the increasingly negative attitude with respect to the New Deal and led Congress to diminish its appropriations for work relief, slowly phasing out its various projects.

The recovery proved to be short-lived. At the end of 1937 the Business Index fell from 110 to 85, bringing the economy back to the state in which it had found itself in 1935. Steel production declined from 80 percent of capacity to 19 percent. Millions of workers lost their jobs once again. The New Deal was now adjudged a dismal failure, and the optimism engendered by it dissipated into general apathy. It seemed that stagnation was now the "normal" state of affairs and that nothing could be done about it. Those who still managed to live reasonably well and, of course, those who profited from the increased productivity of labor felt inclined to make the New Deal responsible for the new downturn and pleaded for giving the market a chance to run its own course.

There was of course the nuisance of the jobless, but their

plight encountered increasing indifference. Society was now prepared to live with them, for, as Harry Hopkins, head of the WPA, explained, people "were bored with the poor, the unemployed and the insecure."[17] This surplus population, it was said with some justice, "does not count in the welfare of the whole population. They are cast out of the groups within the economic system. They have no market for their only economic good, their skill and labor. At present the unemployed constitute a new class in America, and just now they enjoy legal equality with other classes. . . . But with the passing of time the line of demarcation will become more definite. People will be born into this class who never will be employed. The classes inside the economic system will bear children who will not ever be in contact with the group outside the system. . . . The unemployed class will become a class of outcasts. There will be no place for them, no real or fictitious social service they can render. The natural thing for society is to ignore this class and abandon it. It will exist as a nonentity, no one will care what becomes of it. Its members will steal and beg and live in squalor like their brothers in India."[18]

For all practical purposes, by 1938 the New Deal was dead and buried. The economy revived once more, but there were still ten million unemployed in 1939. While total output regained the 1929 level, private investments were still one-third below the level of 1929. Business blamed this situation on high taxes, which accompanied the budget deficits, and on the encroachment of government-induced production on the fields of competitive private investments. Meanwhile, the pragmatically evolved New Deal found a belated theoretical justification in the emerging Keynesian economics. It was now argued that it was not so much the New Deal as its limited application and its inconsistencies that must be held responsible for its apparent failure. "The basic fact was that in 1939," according to Herbert Stein, "the country was unwilling to commit itself to spending as the way to prosperity, especially when the commitment seemed to be permanent. To get out of the 'bottom of the well,' the government would spend as an emergency measure, but it was not prepared to regularize and perpetuate the process."[19]

Keynes's theories were unrelated to the New Deal; in fact,

deficit financing in order to cope with extraordinary government expenditures is as old as and older than capitalism. Since it was always practiced in times of war, it was obvious that it would also be used in the "war" against the depression. Even the idea of the "multiplier effect" of government-induced production made its appearance long before Keynes formulated his theories. But despite the lack of a realistic theory of capital production, the bourgeoisie felt intuitively that government deficit financing may be an effective short-term expedient but could not possibly be a long-term solution. It is clear, of course, that any large-scale investment, from whatever source, will increase production, and that this increase will lead to some additional production apart from the initial investment. But behind the desire for a balanced budget lies the instinctive recognition that a continuous expansion of production by way of government deficit financing must finally destroy the capitalist system.

Of course, the bourgeoisie does not distinguish between production in general and capitalist production. Similarly economics concerns itself with mutually determining flows of abstract incomes and expenditures. If expenditures fall behind incomes, equilibrium is upset but may be restored by compensatory government expenditures. These expenditures must be larger than what is required for the ordinary needs of government, which are met by taxation. The balancing deficit is realized through borrowings on the capital market and turns into the national debt. It is assumed, however, or at least hoped, that government-induced production through deficit financing will revivify the economy and increase incomes sufficiently to yield more taxes and more savings and thus eliminate the earlier deficit. It was then a question not of balancing the budget from year to year but of balancing it over the whole of the business cycle, the deficits of the depression years being compensated by surpluses of the prosperous ones, meanwhile increasing employment and stabilizing economic activities.

It was the expectation of the "pump-priming" effect of government expenditures which induced the New Dealers to adhere to both deficit financing and the principle of the balanced budget; it was only that the balancing of the budget had to be continuously postponed, while fear of the increasing public debt set a low ceiling to the latter. With the disappointments caused by the sluggishness of the recovery, confidence in government-induced production was lost, even on the part of Roosevelt, and more attention was paid to the expansion needs of private enterprise. Although relentlessly practiced, the bourgeois mind refuses to admit that it is not the mere increase of social production but only the increase of the profitability of capital which can lead the private-enterprise system out of the depression. If there is no parallel increase of profits, government expenditures, which are by nature nonprofitable, can only deepen the depression despite all the multiplier effects of an increased production. This does not mean that the "pump" of private capital production remains dry in spite of all the priming done by government. It means that only under particular and favorable conditions will the "priming" have a positive effect. In most cases it will be detrimental to private enterprise and finds its limitation in the capitalist system itself.

In any case the Keynesian theory found no verification in the New Deal. The depression was finally ended not by a new prosperity but through World War II, that is, through the colossal destruction of capital on a worldwide scale and a restructuring of the world economy that assured the profitable expansion of capital for another period. National solutions to the economic crisis had everywhere failed, but by attempting such solutions, the capitalist world system, already shaken to its foundations, had still further deteriorated. Imperialistic solutions were now the order of the day, not least because of the quasi-autarchic antidepression measures that preceded the war. Governmental interventions in the economy are restricted to the nation but affect the world at large and find their limits both at home and abroad. At some point the government-induced expansion of profitless production comes into conflict with the narrowing profit base of capital and plunges the nation into even deeper decline. This is the point at which the imperialist solution seems to be the only way to secure the national capital at the expense of other capitalist nations. An accentuated economic nationalism precedes the international conflicts, even where it serves, at first, no more than the recovery needs of the capitalist nation-state. The New Deal, too, tried to overcome the depression in relative isolation from the decaying world economy, only to partake in its further disruption. With the Spanish Civil War the alignment of the imperialistic forces began to take shape, and the eventuality of a new global war began to agitate the world. Government-induced production became armaments production; in the United States this took the form of an enlarged naval program. The actual outbreak of war turned America into the "arsenal of democracy," but it took America's entry into the war to overcome the Depression and to reach the goal of full employment. Death, the greatest of all the Keynesians, now ruled the world once more.

Notes

1. For instance, Thorstein Veblen, *The Theory of Business Enterprise,* 1904, and Wesley C. Mitchell, *Business Cycles,* 1927.

2. *Wilson Papers,* vol. 4, p. 229.

3. As quoted in R. Goldston, *The Great Depression,* 1968, p. 24.

4. *The Commercial and Financial Chronicle,* 1930, no. 131.

5. H. Hoover, *State Papers,* vol. 2, p. 46.

6. Address of President Hoover on Unemployment Relief, October, 1931, p. 3.

7. As quoted in W. E. Leuchtenburg, *Franklin D. Roosevelt and the New Deal,* 1963, p. 21.

8. G. Kolko, *Main Currents in American History,* 1976, p. 185.

9. F. Freidel, *FDR – Launching the New Deal,* 1973, p. 503.

10. *The Public Papers and Addresses of Franklin D. Roosevelt,* vol. 2, p. 11.

11. E. E. Calkins, "The Will to Recovery," *Current History,* August 1935, p. 454.

12. *The New York Times,* January 2, 1938.

13. *The New Deal,* by the Editors of the *Economist,* 1937, p. 28.

14. R. G. Tugwell, *The Battle of Democracy,* 1935, p. 213.

15. G. Martin, *Madam Secretary Frances Perkins,* 1976, p. 264.

16. *Technical Trends and National Policy,* 1937, p. 87.

17. "The Future of Relief," *The New Republic,* 90:1937, p. 8.

18. A. Rockelt, "The Rise of the Outcasts in America," *Social Science,* Fall 1936, p. 356.

19. *The Fiscal Revolution in America,* 1969, p. 122.

1978

About the Author

Paul Mattick was born in Germany in 1904 and came to the United States in 1926. From 1934 to 1943 he edited the journals *Living Marxism* and *New Essays*. He has contributed numerous articles to scholarly and political journals in Europe, South America, and the United States and is the author of *Marx and Keynes, Crises and Theories of Crises, The Neo-Marxists, Anti-Bolshevik Communism,* and *Unemployment in the United States.*